Surviving Your
Teaching Practice

Surviving Your Teaching Practice

Phil Spencer

McGraw Hill · Open University Press

Open University Press
McGraw-Hill Education
McGraw-Hill House
Shoppenhangers Road
Maidenhead
Berkshire
England
SL6 2QL

email: enquiries@openup.co.uk
world wide web: www.openup.co.uk

and Two Penn Plaza, New York, NY 10121-2289, USA

First published 2011

A catalogue record of this book is available from the British Library

ISBN-13: 978-0-33-523723-4 (pb)
ISBN-10: 0-33-523723-1 (pb)

Library of Congress Cataloging-in-Publication Data
CIP data applied for

Typeset by Aptara Inc., India
Printed in the UK by Bell and Bain Ltd, Glasgow.

Mixed Sources
Product group from well-managed
forests and other controlled sources
www.fsc.org Cert no. TT-COC-002769
© 1996 Forest Stewardship Council

FSC

*The **McGraw·Hill** Companies*

I would like to dedicate this book to my wife Margaret and my children Tom and Kate for their continual love and support. I would also like to thank the trainee teachers, the school-based mentors and the pupils at the various schools which I work with whose experiences have helped to shape this book's outcome.

Education is not about the filling of a bucket, but the lighting of a fire.

W.B. Yeats

Contents

Preface   *xi*

Part I PROFESSIONAL ATTRIBUTES

1 Using this book   3

2 Professionalism   7

3 Preparing for teaching practice   13

4 Relationships   19

5 The QTS Standards explained   28

6 Time management   34

7 Reflective practice   44

8 Formative and summative reviews   55

9 Visits and observations   62

10 Dealing with failure   70

Part II PROFESSIONAL SKILLS

11 Lesson planning   91

12 Assessment of students' work   110

13 Teaching and learning using ICT   121

14 Coping with assignments   129

15 What next?   137

Appendix: The QTS Standards   *144*
Index   *149*

Preface

It would be reasonable to assume that, because you are reading this book, you have already enrolled on a teacher training course and may well be about to start your first teaching practice. You should be keen, excited, a little apprehensive or even scared about what lies ahead of you. If you are not, then you are very unusual! This book is intended to help you get through your teaching practice successfully. Although this book will give you some tips on teaching and assessment in Part II, its main focus are those issues outside the main teaching arena such as relationships, time management and preparing for reviews. This book is about you, the trainee, and it is hoped that the guidance that this book gives you will make you a more effective and intuitive individual who will become a better teacher.

A number of the topics in this book should be covered in your academic time at university. But as we all know, there may be other things on your mind in lectures and so you may not take in everything that was said. The good thing about a book is that you can come back to it when you are ready and in a position to take in what it says. That vital piece of information which you missed will be here and not lost forever. In terms of the QTS standards, this book looks at those issues covered in the Professional Attributes section, i.e. standards 1 to 9, and at the start of each chapter the standards which are particularly relevant are indicated.

You will have decided to become a teacher for a variety of reasons, from a desire to pass your knowledge on to others to the somewhat ill-informed belief that you have lots of time off for holidays! Please be under no illusion that teaching is an easy job, it is not. It is tiring, stressful, time-consuming and sometimes a frustrating rollercoaster which, once you are on, is difficult to get off. There are many experiences which you will have for which may not feel prepared. Children may take you into their confidence with problems which you may not have experienced or they may share their joys with you. If this is the case, then you are a privileged individual to have been so trusted. It is a hard profession and you will need your own support mechanisms to help you through it, but, if you get it right, it is also the most rewarding of jobs, and one which I, for one, have no regrets about choosing.

One of the key messages of this book is about reflection as an individual and as a professional and it is an area to which we return a number of times. It is something we all do, whether as an internal activity or one shared with friends and family. I hope to show you how to use this activity to your advantage and to feed into your teaching practice.

Part I deals with professional attributes that you should acquire, such as a sense of professionalism. Part II deals with professional skills required. These reflect the focus of the QTS Standards.

Part I

Professional Attributes

Using this book

Contents

- Who are the educators? Who can I learn from?
- Using this book
- Chapter outcomes

Learning objectives

By the end of this chapter you will be able to:

- Identify your educators
- Identify your needs and prioritize them
- Identify which order you will use the book
- Set an achievable timetable for the chapters you will be using
- Feel in control and have a purpose.

Who are the educators? Who can I learn from?

One of the key questions to ask yourself is, who will you be learning from, who are your educators? In your teaching practice, you may find that there are a number of these, all of whom are important to you and all of whom will help you to be a better teacher.

Let's be honest, at the start of your teaching practice you may not have a clue what is going to happen to you when you get in front of a classroom full of students. I have seen individuals whose confidence in normal life goes to pieces trying to explain the basics of a piece of software to a class of 12-year-olds! You need all the help you can get and it's not just from your university tutor or your school mentor. You will no doubt have a senior liaison tutor who has responsibility for all the student teachers in your placement school. This person will be a senior teacher with a number of years experience. There will be other classroom teachers too and not just the ones in your area or year. Then there are classroom assistants who will work in a range of subject areas, technicians who have to deal with the students in various ways, and other support staff as well as the students themselves! There may be people outside the teaching profession who may, in some way, present you with ideas which you may not have considered. Be open to these influences. You can learn from everyone in some way, *everyone* is your educator.

There is a huge range of literature which you may also wish to refer to. It is not my intention to make this book a particularly academic one, but rather one which draws on experience, but I will make suggestions for further reading as appropriate at the end of chapters. Don't expect to find all the answers in the books. There is no substitute for experience, but the ideas here may make you consider things which you have not thought of before.

Using this book

Relationships with individuals and groups and understanding such things as reflection are dealt with later in this book. What is needed now is a better understanding of how to use the book. The first thing to understand is that my aim is to write the book in as conversational manner as possible, the questions asked are addressed directly to you. The answers you give are therefore yours. It is a *personal* thing which you may, or may not decide to share with anyone else. What I would encourage you to do, however, is to write things down rather than commit them to memory as it is useful to reflect on what you have thought and the reasons why you thought them at the time. To this end, I suggest that you get your own notebook to write your thoughts in. It's an important book. Your thoughts are valuable in their own right, so treat them as such. Buy yourself a book that feels right to you, that feels special, that you will be happy to use. Make a promise to yourself that you will not scribble anything out or remove any pages. Your journal is part of your journey – you will find it invaluable to look back on your thoughts later.

I would also recommend that you use the journal to note down your thoughts and feelings about what has happened to you in the day – how you felt, how you were challenged, how you dealt with that challenge and what your successes were, and there will be more of these than you realize! It may seem like a time-consuming thing to do but set a little time aside for yourself at the end of the day and write down your thoughts and feelings.

Using this book effectively means that you will therefore have to be active and not passive. I hope that it provokes thought and that you read, reflect and return to it as your placement progresses.

By entering the teaching profession, you will be working with children and adults all day, every day, so it's not a profession for an introverted person. Therefore it is reasonable to assume that you are a fairly outgoing person who can communicate well. It is also reasonable to assume that you want to be the best teacher that you can be, to be like that teacher who inspired you and others. Because of that, you will need to be reflective, to look at what you have done and think 'how could I improve on that?' It is better to start this process at home or in a place where you feel comfortable and safe, where you have space and time and the ability to write your thoughts down. You may wish to do some of these exercises by yourself and some in a group – it's up to you.

As indicated earlier, this book will pose questions for you and, if you wish to use this book to its full potential, you should be actively answering them and attempting to understand your answers and what has informed them. Here is the first activity which is a ranking activity which should only take a few minutes.

Each chapter has tasks to be completed by you and you should write the answers in your journal, to keep as a record of your progress.

Each chapter also refers to the relevant Qualified Teacher Status (QTS) Standard that you should be thinking about evidencing. The Appendix on pp. 146–150 details all the Standards in full. Refer to this before you read the chapter.

Task 1.1

Rank the following statements from 1–10, with 10 being fully confident and 1 being either unsure or having no understanding of the question. This will help you to prioritize and focus in your preparation for your practice.

Question	Mark (1–10)
I am fully prepared for my placement.	
I am fully aware of what I have to do to achieve QTS.	
I understand my relationships within the school.	
I understand the ideas of work–life balance.	
I am clear about continual professional development.	
I understand what is meant by reflection and how it will inform my placement.	
I know what happens in visits and observations.	
I am comfortable in dealing with failure.	
I know about the review process.	

This activity should allow you to think about what preparation you need before your placement and identify which task you may need to tackle first.

Task 1.2

You will need to put your answers from Task 1.1 in order, starting from those marked with the lowest ranking to the highest (1 to 10). This may be the way in which you use this book, although you may wish to use it in another way depending on the situation you are in. For example, you may already be in school and at a point when you are being visited by your university tutor.

Chapter	Rank

I do not feel that it is practical or feasible to tackle this list in Task 1.2 all in one go. It may also be counter-productive as you may not be able to dedicate the time to it which it deserves. You need to prioritize and to think about the time you have to allocate to the tasks. In an ideal world, you will have started this process before you are on practice, but you may already be there. Either way, you need to be organized to be effective, especially at the start of your teaching career where your inexperience may result in things taking longer than they would be to an experienced teacher. One handy tip is get a diary or journal now and get used to using it. Identify your lowest ranking chapter and confirm that this is the one which you need to tackle first. Once you have done this, decide when would be a good time to start on the chapter, what time you intend to allocate to it and write this in. Make a promise to yourself that this is what you will do. Start off as you mean to go on and make sure that the time that you allocate to each of your tasks is reasonable and achievable. Good luck!

Chapter outcomes

You should now feel more confident in your ability to identify who your educators are in this process. You should also have a good idea of what your needs are and be able to prioritize them, although you will have to accept that these priorities are likely to change as your practice progresses. You may have an idea of the order in which you will use the book and have set a timetable for the chapters you are going to be using. Hopefully, you should also be feeling in control and have a sense of direction and purpose.

2 Professionalism

Contents

- Defining professionalism in the school context
- Professionalism and dress
- Professionalism and language
- Professionalism in the community
- Professionalism and social networking
- Professionalism and timekeeping
- Professionalism and communication
- Summary
- Further reading

Learning objectives

By the end of this chapter, you will have a better understanding of:

- What it means to be a professional within the teaching profession
- What is expected in terms of your own professional conduct.

QTS Standards

The chapter is particularly relevant to Q Standards 1, 2, 3, 4, 6, 7 and 9.

Relationships with children and young people

Q1 Have high expectations of children and young people including a commitment to ensuring that they can achieve their full educational potential and to establishing fair, respectful, trusting, supportive and constructive relationships with them.

Q2 Demonstrate the positive values, attitudes and behaviour they expect from children and young people.

Frameworks

Q3 (a)   Be aware of the professional duties of teachers and the statutory framework within which they work.

Q3 (b)   Be aware of the policies and practices of the workplace and share in collective responsibility for their implementation.

Communicating and working with others

Q4   Communicate effectively with children, young people, colleagues, parents and carers.

Q6   Have a commitment to collaboration and co-operative working.

Personal professional development

Q7 (a)   Reflect on and improve their practice, and take responsibility for identifying and meeting their developing professional needs.

Q7 (b)   Identify priorities for their early professional development in the context of induction.

Q9   Act upon advice and feedback and be open to coaching and mentoring.

Task 2.1

If you were to describe someone as professional, what would you mean?

Thinking back to your school days, who among the teaching staff had the respect of both staff and students alike? What were they like?

What do you expect of someone who is dealing with impressionable young people?

Defining professionalism in the school context

One of the things which you will hear your university tutor and school mentor refer to many times is the issue of professionalism. Therefore this is clearly important and in fact the first nine QTS standards are all about professionalism. But what exactly does this mean for you as a trainee teacher? In terms of a definition, professionalism could be described as high standards of professional ethics, behaviour and work while carrying out one's profession. It's about how you as an individual act and present yourself while you are on practice and later when you have qualified. In addition to this, it's also about how you conduct yourself outside the workplace. This definition would be supported by Pope and Shilvock (2008, p. 15) who also point out that maintaining professionalism at all times may be difficult and frustrating, especially when faced with students and staff. However, they also stress the importance of consistency in the way that you conduct yourself.

We should start with the basic premise that you as a teacher are expected to be a role model for your students. You are expected to exhibit those sorts of behaviours which you would expect from a person in a position of considerable responsibility. Your mentors can excuse a lesson going poorly or making some basic errors in the production of resources, but they will not forgive lateness to a lesson, phoning in sick because your social life has got in the way of your better judgement or turning up to lessons dressed inappropriately. When you are in a school, you are no longer an undergraduate turning up for a lecture. You are expected to be able to take the responsibility for other people's learning as well as your own.

Professionalism and dress

Consequently, professionalism, the way you act and the way you dress, is very much under your own control. If you think that these things are petty and irrelevant to your ability to teach, then you are mistaken, they are at the heart of it. And the way that you present yourself is the first thing that you can take control of.

I recently put the question of the importance of dress to a head teacher whose comment was that he was: 'looking for people who present themselves well in the clothing sense of the word' (B. Hunter, Head Teacher, Hope Valley School). I found this comment to be no surprise. It is reasonable to expect a certain standard of dress from any member of staff for the message that it conveys to fellow professionals. However, I thought that it was important to follow this up by posing a similar question to students whom I had observed in schools. Here are some of their comments.

> If they were in jeans or a tracksuit, I would not take them seriously.
> (Tom S, Y7, Bradfield School, March 2010)
>
> They should look like a teacher, smart.
> (Becky B, Y8, Yarbourough School, March 2010)
>
> We have to wear a uniform and look smart, so should they.
> (Casey F, Y10, Dearne High School, March 2010)
>
> If they look presentable, you take more notice of them.
> (Hannah T, Y10, Hope Valley School, April 2010)

I was expecting comments along the line of 'it does not matter, so long as they are nice' but only one student out of the 20 that I asked responded in this way. So it would appear that it's not just the staff whom you need to impress, the students have standards too.

For the gents, it means that you will be expected to wear a collar and tie and that jeans are totally out. Now gentlemen may say at this point, 'I hate wearing a tie', as some of my current trainees have said, and others may say that it is a potential hazard, especially for technology teachers. To the former, I would say, 'Accept it and get on with it', the students may not like their uniform, but they are expected to wear it. I accept the issue of the tie and health and safety but this can always be tucked in when operating machinery, so it's just common sense on that one. Basically students, fellow teachers, parents and anyone else who you will be dealing with at school will treat you differently if you are in a collar and tie than if you are not. You may not like it but it is a simple fact borne out by years of experience as a teacher and a mentor.

For the ladies, again, it is an issue of being sensible about things. You will be expected to dress conservatively for the most part, but let's be honest; we are there to teach rather than going out to a club. You will be dealing with young children and in some cases with young adults who will be looking at you all the time. Skirts cannot be too short and tops must not be too low. If you choose to dress other than this, then you do so at your peril.

In both cases, personal jewellery should be kept to a minimum. I have seen numerous arguments between staff and their pupils over this issue. Staff telling pupils to remove their large earrings when they are wearing them seems unreasonable and the obvious argument from a pupil of 'Well, you are wearing them' is pretty justifiable. I have worn a silver bracelet for years, it's one of the first things I put on when I am not in school mode but at school it is never there. I would not expect the pupils to follow the school rules if I was happy to flaunt them myself. Do not undermine yourself before you start.

Professionalism and language

Your behaviour in the classroom itself is an issue. You need to be careful with the way you speak. You must *never* swear in front of pupils. You have to be careful with your opinions, especially on contentious topics. Your pupils will rapidly lose respect for you if you are seen to be someone who is sloppy with the way you speak. You also need to keep an even temperament and not shout at the students all the time. How would the pupils feel if the person who was supposed to be in charge of them was not in charge of themselves? You are there before the students and you are prepared at all times. For some, this will prove difficult at first, but it is vital for all teachers. Although time management is something which I will be dealing with later on in this book, it is appropriate to raise this topic briefly below.

Professionalism in the community

Once outside school, well, that's a different thing, isn't it? It's nothing to do with school what I do in my spare time. *Wrong!* Outside school, you are still a member of the community whose profession commands respect. Could you imagine what would happen to your reputation with staff and students if you were arrested for fighting at a football match or if you were seen drunk by a parent or, worse still, a student? We all need to let our hair down but you have to think about how and where you do it. If you are a younger trainee and you are in a local club and a sixth form student comes in, the smart thing to do would be for you to leave.

Professionalism and social networking

Connected to this is the use of social networking sites such as 'Facebook', a very popular part of current culture. However, for the teacher, it's full of potential hazards. Let's be honest, if you were a pupil and you have a new teacher, wouldn't this be one of the first places you would go to find some information? What joy if you not only found a site but then managed to get some personal information or even an embarrassing photo of your new teacher socializing! Put yourself in the shoes of the pupil and think what they might do with this information. A few photos can have a huge impact on your standing or even your ability to get a post in the first place. One of my own trainees recently had the offer of an interview rescinded after the head teacher had searched the internet for any information on the candidate. The lesson is clear – keep clear of social networking sites.

Professionalism and timekeeping

It seems odd to have to write about this one, as some things just seem obvious, but your punctuality and timekeeping are also something which is hugely important. Many schools start with a briefing session before the school day starts fully. You need to make sure that you are always there and always early for it, never late. You also need to make sure that you are there for the full school day. If you have a free period at the end of the day, this is not a reason for leaving the school. Nor should you be in the car park at the end of the school day trying to get out before the pupils. Although the official day may end, the impression given by a rapid getaway every day tends to be that of a lack of commitment. Obviously, there may be some reason for this, such as child care, but if there is not, then do not do it. The following quote sums the situation up from the mentor's point of view:

> What I need is a clear demonstration of commitment from trainees. Ones who arrive just in time at the start of the day and get out as quick as they can at the end of the day do not create a good impression.
>
> (Mentor B, Sheffield, Jan. 2010)

Connected with this is making appointments in school time. In some situations, such as hospital appointments or an interview for a job, there may be no option for you. But making appointments in school time should be avoided if at all possible. If you are not here, someone will have to cover your class. Your convenience may be someone else's inconvenience.

Professionalism and communication

Whatever happens, if you are going to be late, if you do have to make an appointment, if something has happened which may come out in school and have a negative impact, let your mentor know immediately. Failing to keep your mentor informed is simply not acceptable and will have a catastrophic impact on your relationship with them. You also need to communicate any other issues of importance within the department from phone calls to messages from other members of staff. It extends further to any incidents in the classroom such as behavioural issues or students falling behind with coursework. You are only there for a short time and when you leave, the host teachers will have to pick up from where you left off. The effective running of a department depends on clear communication and failure to pass on information can affect this.

Summary

You should now have a better understanding of what we mean by professionalism within teaching and what will be expected of you in terms of your dress, general conduct and communication. Remember, you will be responsible for the education of others, and education is not just about your subject, you are a role model for the students in your care. As we see from this chapter, your professionalism and professional judgement have to extend beyond the classroom and the working day and reach out into your own private life. By being professional in your everyday life, you can demonstrate to your students how to behave in an acceptable manner. This goes a long way to earning the respect of not only the students, but also parents, carers and colleagues alike.

Further reading

Arthur, J., Davison, J. and Lewis, M. (2005) *Professional Values and Practice: Achieving the Standards for QTS*. London: RoutledgeFalmer.

Denby, N. (2008) *How to Achieve your QTS: A Guide for Students*. London: Sage.

Dymoke, S. and Harrison, J. (2008) *Reflective Teaching and Learning: A Guide to Professional Issues for Beginning Secondary Teachers*. London: Sage.

Pope, M. and Shilvock, K. (2008) *Successful Teaching Placements: Secondary*. Exeter: Learning Matters.

3 | Preparing for teaching practice

Contents

- Your practice expectations
- The practical issues
- Finding out about the school
- Contacting the school
- Getting to the school
- The first day – making the right impressions
- Summary

Learning objectives

In this chapter I will be looking at preparing yourself for your teaching practice. This will include:

- Finding out about your placement school
- Contacting the school
- Getting to school
- The first day at school.

QTS Standards

This chapter is particularly relevant to Q Standards 3a and 7b.

Frameworks

Q3 (a) Be aware of the professional duties of teachers and the statutory framework within which they work.

Personal and professional development

Q7 (b) Identify priorities for their early professional development in the context of induction.

Task 3.1

What do you expect from your first teaching practice?

How do you think you will be perceived by the staff and the students?

How much of what is perceived is in your control and how much is beyond it?

Your practice expectations

As with every teacher training course, there are times when you will be at university and there will be times when you are on placement. Your expectations of what to do in these environments will of course vary considerably. While at university, you are the student, attending your sessions and expecting someone else to deliver to you. Apart from hitting your targets in terms of assignment deadlines and other course tasks, you tend not to have many responsibilities as such. You will tend to be more relaxed, you may see it as a chance to socialize to some degree, you will work, but without others having expectations of you. You may even grumble about getting to your lectures on time or if a tutor questions you about missing a session. University is where you will get your theoretical knowledge; school is where you have to put the theory into practice.

Your experience at school will be totally different than at university. The university is interested in assessing your theoretical understanding. Your tutors will not be overly concerned at how you dress, for example, it's not important to them. At school, it's very different. You will be expected to behave in a professional manner, to dress and speak accordingly, be punctual, be a role model to your charges. At school, you are being assessed all the time – by your mentors, your work colleagues, parents, pupils, in fact, all the members of the school community. Some trainees find this difficult at first. This is particularly true for the young trainee who was in school until a relatively short time ago, as well as for the more mature student who has not had to deal with young students, their needs and behaviour and whose expectations may be based on their own education experiences 20 years before. Everyone is apprehensive and nervous when they go to a new school, an experienced teacher can be equally nervous when meeting a new class for the first time. We will deal with the issue of meeting your class for the first time later; however, it is important to think about the experience of preparing for your placement early on.

Your teaching placements will put you in front of a highly critical and at times unforgiving audience. You may well find out a great deal about yourself which you did not know before the placement started. New strengths may develop, old uncertainties reappear and how you deal with these issues is a personal journey for all. However, I guarantee that you will be a different person at the end of your first placement from the one who started it. Many of your

initial expectations and concerns will have been addressed. You will be aware of what you may need to work on in your second placement; you will be able to see your gaps. The end of your first placement is a very good time to reflect if teaching is for you. For most people the answer will be 'yes', and they will embrace their next placement with enthusiasm. Whatever stage you are at, though, it is worth taking some time out to think about several key things such as:

- What is your comfort zone?

- What takes you out of your comfort zone?

- How self-aware are you?

- What are your main concerns about your placement?

- What do you consider your strengths and areas for development are?

- What do you think the school's expectations of you are?

- What do you think that the school will be expecting you to do?

The practical issues

As well as the personal and emotional issues which you need to consider, there are also the more mundane, practical issues. In most cases, the university will allocate a school to you which may be based upon a number of things such as your previous experience, a knowledge of the person you are and the type of schools who have offered placements, the depth of support you may need or the strength and experience of the mentor. This whole experience is a partnership between you, the school and the university. It is in no one's interest to turn out weak teachers and so we must all work together to get the best that we can. In some instances, your mentor may be new and may be being mentored themselves, but more likely, the mentor will have had a number of trainees over the years and will bring lots of experience to the learning process.

One point which I would like to stress concerning the placement is that you should avoid a placement close to where you live and your house should definitely not be within the catchment area. The advantages of convenience will be outweighed considerably by the disadvantages of the students knowing where you live and where you socialize. It's one thing occasionally bumping into a student in a shopping centre but quite another to have them living on the same street. It is also a good idea to avoid a placement in a school which has a relative in it. You need to stand on your own two feet as an individual and relatives can make this difficult at times.

Finding out about the school

When you have been given details of your placement school, you will be keen to find out more about it. There are many ways to find out more information.

The first and most obvious point of call would be via OfSTED where you could look at the site and download the latest report. While this may be informative in many ways in terms of grading a school on its performance, it may not give a full picture of the school. Most schools now have a website which will give you a considerable amount of information about life in the school, its staff, its extracurricular activities and so forth which is obviously a good way to get a feel for the school itself. The local press is also a good way to gain information as the schools often tend to use the press to publicize their successes wherever possible.

I am a great advocate of visiting the area surrounding the school to get a feel for the local environment. This may be as simple as driving round the area or walking around it. Either way, it is a good way to get a 'feel' for the area and some of the issues which may face the school.

The worst thing to do is to simply turn up to your placement with no idea of the school and its catchment area. It displays a lack of interest and possibly a lack of commitment on your behalf.

Contacting the school

When you get the details of your school, write to your mentor immediately. It creates a great impression if they receive a covering letter and an up-to-date CV. It also helps the mentor in shaping your timetable as they can match your skills to the groups which you are likely to teach. If you get the opportunity, you may also contact the school to ask if you can come to have a look around the school before you start. This will not only be informative for you but also show your mentor that you are committed and keen. In terms of what not to do, do not turn up unannounced and also make sure that you do not make any contact with students at the school via internet gaming sites, for example.

Getting to the school

You will also need to find out how to get to the school in a more practical way. Obviously, if you have a car, find the best route to the school and do a trial run. See how long it takes in terms of time and distance and make sure that you add some time on to take traffic into account. Do not think that the time for the first run will be the time that it takes you to get there on a school day. Driving on a Saturday afternoon is going to be different from 7:30 on a Monday morning. I have seen many students try this and miss briefing on their first day as a result. Always build some time in – it is much better to arrive early than late.

If you have to take public transport to get to the school, again, make sure that you do a trial run to make sure you understand the time that it will take to get to and from school. Find out the time of the bus that will get you to

school on time without sharing it with the pupils if at all possible. It is much better and more comfortable for you to arrive before them than with them.

There may be some who choose to cycle to work. While I applaud your commitment to both your personal well-being and that of our planet, try to ensure that you have access to some appropriate working clothes when you get there and, if at all possible, make sure you get a shower. No one likes a smelly teacher!

The first day – making the right impressions

Well, you have contacted your mentor with your details, you have done your dummy run to find out how to get to your school and you have found out all the information on the school that you can. Now it's time to go to school! First, refer back to Chapter 2 on professionalism and think about how you look. That is the first thing that the staff will notice and comment upon, so make sure that you are well presented and well groomed. Make sure that you arrive in plenty of time and that you report to reception accordingly.

There is a good chance that you will be one of a number of trainees who have arrived at the school, and you will all be feeling nervous, wondering what is expected of you, what your mentor is like, and probably most importantly, what the class will be like. If this is your first placement, you are likely to feel considerably more nervous than your second or even third one. Trust me, it will be fine.

Task 3.2

If you were the mentor, how would you feel about meeting your new trainee?

What do you think the mentor wants out of this experience?

How do you expect to feel on the first day?

What are your expectations of the first day?

In most cases, the first week in the school will be an induction where you can be expected to be bombarded with facts, figures and policies from a range of people from around the school including the head teacher, SENCO, the senior liaison tutor who has direct links with the university, and so on. It is not unknown for some trainees not to see their mentor or department other than in passing when taken around the school by staff or students. Although this can be tiring, please make sure that you look interested at all times and that you ask questions as you go. Yawning and slumping down on a chair do not create a good impression to someone who is taking the time to show you around their school. What I can guarantee is that you will be the talk of the staffroom at the end of the day and it's up to you what they say!

Summary

After reading this chapter, I now hope that you have a better understanding of how to prepare for your teaching practice. It is hugely important not only to consider the practical issues of how to get there and when to get there, but also to consider the importance of the impression you give when you arrive at your school. Remember the relationships you form with the staff on this first day will set the tone for the practice, and setting a bad impression is not an option for you.

4 | Relationships

Contents

- Your school mentor
- Your university tutor
- Your students
- Your colleagues
- Non-teaching and support staff
- Other trainee teachers
- Mistakes and problems
- Summary
- Further reading

Learning objectives

I have always viewed the relationships which you build in teaching as the area which can make or break your experience. By the end of this chapter I hope you will be able to understand your:

- Relationships with staff both inside and outside your teaching practice
- Relationships with your fellow trainees
- Relationships with your students
- Some common problems which you may experience in your teaching practice.

QTS Standards

This chapter is particularly relevant to Q Standards 1, 2, 3, 4, 5, 6 and 9.

Relationships with children and young people

Q1 Have high expectations of children and young people including a commitment to ensuring that they can achieve their full educational potential and to establishing fair, respectful, trusting, supportive and constructive relationships with them.

Q2 Demonstrate the positive values, attitudes and behaviour they expect from children and young people.

Frameworks

Q3 (a) Be aware of the professional duties of teachers and the statutory framework within which they work.

Q3 (b) Be aware of the policies and practices of the workplace and share in collective responsibility for their implementation.

Communicating and working with others

Q4 Communicate effectively with children, young people, colleagues, parents and carers.

Q5 Recognise and respect the contribution that colleagues, parents and carers can make to the development and well-being of children and young people and to raising their levels of attainment.

Q6 Have a commitment to collaboration and co-operative working.

Personal and Professional Development

Q9 Act upon advice and feedback and be open to coaching and mentoring.

Task 4.1

Before we start, I would like you to ask yourself what you think constitutes a good relationship. It may help you to split this into different areas. Think of this as relationships which may be with your friends/supporters; relationships with professionals; relationships with people you are responsible for; and relationships with those responsible for you.

Second, think of these same groups and think about what it would mean to have a negative impact on these relationships.

Your school mentor

Your relationship with your school mentor is key to your success on placement. It is because of this that some trainees approach this area with some trepidation, asking the question 'What if my mentor does not like me?' While this is a valid question, you also have to ask yourself: 'What can I do to make sure that the mentor likes me, or at the very least, is happy to work alongside me?' One of the main things that you can do to ensure that your working relationship is a good one is to make sure that you are professional at all times as identified in Chapter 2. You will need to be keen, hard-working, enthusiastic, willing to take on a challenge and to push yourself forward in school life. You also need to be willing to accept and act upon criticism from your mentor (see standard Q9).

But let's look at it from the mentor's point of view. What does the mentor get out of this relationship? Do they have trainees by choice or are they pressurized into this? Do they feel comfortable in the role? Are they willing to give the hard advice when it is needed? Well, for the vast part, mentors are more than happy to have trainees and have opted in to the programme as they see it as important for the development of themselves and future staff. In some cases, it also gives them the opportunity to see potential new staff. However, the relationship with a mentor can be a tricky one. First, there is their existing role within the school. A mentor may have a wide range of responsibilities to deal with and the chances that they are only a classroom teacher will be small. Someone who has the responsibility for a trainee will usually have considerable experience, may well be a head of department and in some instances be on the senior leadership team of the school. They will certainly have their own teaching load and, in secondary school, most will have a form with all the work this presents. Taking on a trainee certainly adds to the workload but will be done nevertheless – always remember that.

You may find that your mentor has to maintain an element of distance from you and you may find this to be a little off-putting. I have certainly had conversations with my trainees who have been concerned that their mentor seems to be 'standoffish'. This is a little bit of self-defence on the part of the mentor. Put yourself in their position. They have a new person, who they know little about and have no control over their selection, about to be teaching their pupils in their school. Their main priority will not be the trainee, it will be the impact that you will have on their pupils, with whom they will have built up relationships and may well be guiding towards qualifications. In short, they will be taking a risk on you working with their students. If it all goes wrong, you will leave and they will have to pick up the pieces. Is it any wonder that they may feel a little defensive? There is also the situation that you are working in. They are there to help you through your placement, but what if it doesn't go the way you expected? What if they have to recommend that you should not progress or have to give you a 'cause for concern' rating? What if there is a discipline issue to resolve? The relationship between the trainee and the mentor is a difficult one for the mentor. They have to be your teacher, your colleague and your boss all rolled into one! Obviously, they will want to be friends but they cannot push it too far in case they have to make a difficult decision. They are, after all, guardians of the profession and they have a responsibility to make sure that only those who are up to the job are allowed to qualify.

In terms of what you can expect from the relationship, first and foremost, it's support and guidance. If you have a problem, or need some help, this person is the first port of call in your teaching practice. You will not arrive at the school, be given a timetable and told to get on with it until you return to university. You can expect your mentor to be with you all the way. In a more formal setting, you can expect a weekly, timetabled meeting where you can discuss issues which may have arisen during the week, go through any teaching concerns you may have and review your Q standards. This is also a good place to identify targets which you may want to set to meet Q standards.

Your mentor is also responsible for writing the formative and summative assessments of your teaching placements, where strengths and areas for improvements will be documented. The formative and summative assessments are areas of considerable concern for both parties. The trainee wants everything to be 'sunshine and roses' and to be told that they are the best trainee ever, while the mentor dreads giving negative comments. However, like it or not, it is a process which must be done, so it is best to get on with it. You may not hear what you hoped for but you do have to listen to and act upon the suggestions that are made to you. For the most part, trainees will progress through their placements as expected. You should accept that there may be some issues and areas for development; you are only just starting in this career, after all. If the recruitment procedure has been good and the trainee has followed instruction and advice, then failure on a placement is the exception, although it is something which does happen. I will look at the issue of failing a placement later on in this book, it deserves a section of its own and should not be skimmed over.

If you are particularly weak in an area of the standards, you may be given a 'Cause for Concern' (C4C) or similar document which will outline the problem area and will have targets attached to it by the mentor, which must be achieved by a certain date. Receiving a C4C can be stressful but it is not the end of the world. It simply indicates the improvement target as well as steps that you can take to get there and most go no further than that.

Mentors are also responsible for checking that you are collecting the QTS standards which you will need in order to achieve QTS status. In fact, it is your mentor who signs them off at the end of your teaching practice and not your university tutor, which is a common misconception.

What if my mentor doesn't like me?

Your mentor does not have to like you but they do have to be professional in what they do and you have the right to expect this. For the most part, it is this impression that some people tend to give and many trainees fail to recognize this. However, if you feel that there is a real issue, and you do not feel that you can talk to your mentor about it, get in touch with your university tutor immediately and let them know of your concerns. Such situations can be sorted out quickly as they do tend to be misunderstandings, but if the worst comes to the worst, your tutor may be able to move you to a different placement school.

Your university tutor

Your relationship with your university tutor is also vital. In some cases, the university tutor will be the sole person who has also delivered all of your sessions, supported you with tutorials and seminars, marked your assignments and provided feedback to enable you to improve. They will also be the person who comes out to the schools to do observations and may well have a rather large hand in sorting out your placements. Your university tutor will work closely with your school mentor and may well know them personally, having worked with them for years.

They are the connection point between your university life and your teaching placement. Consequently, they need to be kept informed of everything, all of the time. Some trainees make the mistake of thinking that their teaching placements are separate from their university life and what goes on in one has nothing to do with the other. This is a wrong assumption. This process is a partnership and should be treated as such. You will find that your university tutor will be in touch with your mentor via the phone, e-mail, visits and meetings, so they will know what is going on or if there is a problem.

As someone on a professional course, you should also keep your tutor informed of such things as illness, days off for interview, and so forth. I would also expect my students to inform me of any important incidents which have occurred in the school which have impacted on them, for example if a student has made an allegation against a trainee or if there are changes in circumstances at home which have an impact on your ability to perform on the course. This may be, for example, a death or illness in the family. If your tutor does not know, they cannot help you. Of course, you can keep such issues to yourself but if it impacts on others by, for example, not being able to attend school, you have a responsibility to make others aware as soon as possible.

Your students

Task 4.2

Think back to your school days and to a teacher you liked, who inspired you, whom you respected. Think of the qualities they had: what was it about them that made the impression?

Think about a teacher whom you did not like, who turned you off education, whom you least want to be like. What was it about them that made you feel negative?

The pupils you will teach will make your teaching practice; it is as simple as that. Do not expect to like everyone or expect them all to like you – that is unrealistic – but it is important to establish a good working relationship with as many as possible and this is vital to your success as a teacher. Throughout this next section, I want you to reflect on those teachers whom you have just thought about in Task 4.1.

You may have seen the advert for prospective teachers outlining the great list of jobs which they perform in the school from educator, mediator, and entertainer to first aid specialist. Well, it's true! You will have to be all sorts of things to all sorts of people. First and foremost, you have to be *professional* at all times. We have covered professionalism already in Chapter 2, but basically it's about being sensible in your actions. Do not put yourself in situations which may come back to haunt you. For example, you should avoid going into a room by yourself with a student. If you have to be with an individual on their own, make sure that there is another member of staff with you. Do not touch students in any way which could be seen as either overly friendly or hostile. Be careful with the language you use and how you phrase things. These are the obvious ones. Basically you need to maintain a distance from your students, no matter how close you are to them, which you will be especially if you have a form. You will become a big part of their lives and may well see them more than any other adult, including some at home.

So the teacher part is established. Professional at all times, high expectations and a fair approach. But the teachers who get the most respect and the most from their pupils are those who are seen to be willing to go that extra mile, to show that they care and that they are willing to put themselves out for individuals. In short, the ones who look like they are there for more than a job to pay the bills. My advice would be to be personable, find out about each child and their interests and ask about them, get involved in extra-curricular activities, visits and trips to let the students see the human side of you as well. I became involved in coaching rugby, which resulted in me working with some students who could be seen as challenging. I worked on these relationships, enjoying the rugby and seeing the kids develop, and the spin-offs for me were considerable. The odd thing now is that some of the students whom I first coached now play for the senior team whose juniors I now coach and they still come to talk to me and my new team. It's a rewarding feeling.

There is always the question of 'what if pupils get too close?' and I will deal with this later.

Your colleagues

In this section, I will be looking at how you should work with your colleagues. By colleagues, I mean the teaching staff with whom you will be working, which is likely to be members of your department (in the case of secondary) or your whole school (in the case of primary).

The size of this group can vary considerably. If you are in a small rural primary, the school may only have four teaching staff. In a large secondary, the maths department may be as big as 10. Obviously, group dynamics will play a big part in this and the fact that you are a trainee in the school may also have an impact. But the important thing is that you try to get on with and fit in with these people. They may not be directly supervising you in the way that your mentor will, but the mentor will take into account what colleagues think when setting targets and writing reports. You will need to be seen to work with members of this group (a requirement of Q standards 4, 5, 6, 32 and 33) and become a valuable part of the team. As you may well be taking over some of their classes, they will be a valuable source of information and advice as to effective ways to handle the groups.

There may also be a social aspect to this group which may not be open to you with your mentor. My advice would be to embrace this opportunity. If there is a Christmas party or a social event, then join in, but be careful that you do not get too 'social'. I have seen one trainee's reputation fall rather dramatically after choosing the wrong options on a night out with the department with big implications for the remainder of their practice.

Non-teaching and support staff

This group of individuals covers the support staff who you may work with, from the technicians, office staff, cleaners, caretakers and all the other members of the school community. This body of people may be up to half of the total staff and their input into the school is crucial.

You may well work with support staff who are linked directly with a particular student. This person will follow the pupil around all day and will know what makes them tick and how they will behave in different situations. Get to know these people and seek out their help, many of them have seen it all before. It is a good idea to run through lesson plans and individual resources with your support staff if you want to get the most out of your lessons.

Technicians are a very important group of people as far as the classrooms are concerned. In many subjects, such as technology and science, they may be responsible for setting up the classroom and collecting resources for the lessons you teach. In subjects such as ICT, their knowledge in terms of hardware and software may well exceed your own and they are usually willing to advise on the effectiveness of what you are trying to deliver. Many trainees have gone into a lesson and tried to deliver a lesson using a piece of software which will not run on the network. A simple conversation with the technician could have resolved this issue before it arose.

A common error made by trainees, especially young ones, is that there is a clear ranking system within the school and that, although they are on the bottom of the rung in teaching terms, they are above the support staff. *This is simply not the case.* You are on an equal footing with them, so make sure that you treat them with the courtesy and respect that you give to your teaching colleagues, as this will make your teaching practice considerably easier.

Other trainee teachers

Most trainee students will find that they are not the only trainees in their school. In secondary schools, trainees tend to be from the different subjects which the school delivers. So you may have two English students, one maths student, three scientists and a PE student in the same school. You may be from one or a number of teacher training institutions, but you will all be in the same boat and so should be in a position to help each other and in some instances work alongside each other.

Most schools will also have training sessions which run alongside your teaching practice, covering such things as behaviour management within the school, special educational needs (SEN), and so on. Consequently, you will be working together. Good relationships within this group can therefore prove beneficial to all parties.

Mistakes and problems

I made a mistake, what should I do?

There may come a time when you have made a mistake whether that is by saying the wrong thing to a pupil or member of staff, making a twit of yourself at a staff night out, or failing to give a piece of vital information such as the Y11 coursework marks to the exams officer. At times like these, you can feel very stressed and upset indeed. The first thing is not to panic! Whatever it is that you have done, it is likely that others will have done it before you. The worst thing you can do is to try to cover it up, deny it or hide it. You need to inform your mentor immediately of the situation and make sure that you tell them everything that has happened so that they can help you to resolve the situation. For the most part, problems can be solved with a combination of honesty and eating humble pie, but you do have to accept responsibility for your own actions.

It is also a good idea to let your university tutor know of the situation, especially if the problem has impacted on other members of staff at the placement school.

Dealing with the teenage crush

This can be a big problem for some trainees and can have a huge impact upon their decision to remain in the teaching profession. To some people, it can be a cause for some humour, especially for those who are not the target. I have had to deal with trainee students who have been followed home by pupils or more recently one student having his photo taken by year 9 girls. Such actions can impact on classroom control, relationships with colleagues and others and can make your experience a miserable one, so it has to be resolved quickly. First, remember that you are the adult here and must act in a responsible and professional manner. The first thing to do is to flag up your concerns to your mentor. Do not, under any circumstances, keep it to yourself or put yourself into a situation where you may have allegations made against you. Do not try to handle the situation by yourself as this is far too risky an undertaking. It may mean that a member of staff has a word with the pupil(s) concerned to draw a line under the matter, allowing you to carry on your teaching practice without further disturbance.

I have heard of one trainee who met a young lady in a nightclub in the city in which he was studying. Although nothing untoward happened, imagine the trainee's shock when he arrived at his practice school to see the young lady in question in Y11, especially since she had said she was in college! His immediate reaction was the correct one – he informed his mentor immediately of the situation and was withdrawn from the placement by the university. The point is that you have to be very careful with your social life as a trainee teacher.

Summary

After reading this chapter, you should have a better understanding of the importance which relationships have on your successful placement. Your relationships with teaching staff and the wider school community can make or break your experience in schools, so it is vital that you have good relationships across the school. Remember, be professional at all times and work hard at building positive relationships. You may only be in the school for a short time but the legacy that you will leave could be a long one. Also, a considerable number of students get their first posts as a consequence of their teaching practices, and for the school this is the best way to see what a trainee is really like, as a simple interview does not always give the full picture. Finally, remember that even if there is not a post available at the school you are training in, there will be others and your mentor will be writing a reference!

Further reading

Long, R. (2005) *The Art of Positive Communication: A Practitioner's Guide to Managing Behaviour.* London: David Fulton.

Pope, M. and Shilvock, K. (2008) *Successful Teaching Placements: Secondary.* Exeter: Learning Matters.

Rodgers, B. (2006) *Classroom Behaviour.* London: Sage.

5 The QTS Standards explained

Contents

- What are the QTS Standards?
- What constitutes quality evidence?
- Using the same evidence to reference more than one Standard
- The QTS tests
- Summary
- Further reading

Learning objectives

In this chapter we will consider the issue of the QTS Standards. By the end of it, you should have:

- A better understanding of the QTS Standards
- An understanding of what constitutes evidence
- How to cross-refer
- The role of the QTS skills tests.

QTS Standards

This chapter is particularly relevant to Q7 as by identifying and collecting evidence you will also be an active participant in your own professional development from an early stage, rather than letting it be driven by a third party.

Personal and professional development

Q7 (a) Reflect on and improve their practice, and take responsibility for identifying and meeting their developing professional needs.

Q7 (b) Identify priorities for their early professional development in the context of induction.

What are the QTS Standards?

The QTS Standards represent the vehicle through which you will prove that you have evidenced the basic skills which are needed to become a teacher. There are 33 Standards, divided into three sections of Profession Attributes (Q 1–9); Professional Knowledge and Understanding (Q10–22); and Professional Skills (Q23–33). As indicated earlier, one of the key objectives of this book is to help you to understand and focus on the requirements of the professional attributes section. Consequently, although I will also be looking at issues such as lesson preparation, resource development and assessment in its various forms, I will be focusing on Standards 1 to 9. This is not to say that professional skills are not as important as those issues covered in the professional attributes section, as each area is as important as the other. Within each section of the QTS, there are other sub-sections. For example, Standards Q1–9 are divided into Relationships with Children and Young People; Frameworks; Communicating and Working with Others; and Personal and Professional Development. The full 2008 QTS Standards are contained in the Appendix on p. 146.

What constitutes quality evidence?

The amount of evidence gathered, where it is gathered from and how you store it depend upon not only the requirements of the university but also your personal preference. However, the first thing that you must do is to get yourself organized and start this early. You must start gathering quality evidence as soon as it presents itself and not leave it to the final two weeks of your teaching practice. Fortunately there is a good amount of help and guidance available to the trainee and the first port of call which I would recommend is that offered by the TDA, a source often neglected by both the trainee and the mentor, see: http://www.tda.gov.uk/partners/ittstandards/guidance_08/qts.aspx.

As your mentor plays such a huge part in your Standards, it is vital that you involve them from the start to be clear in your mind exactly what your mentor expects. Mentors have the responsibility for checking the evidence that you have gathered for QTS Standards and, in the final instance, signing them off as met or otherwise. Your university tutor will no doubt want to check the progress of your files but, to be honest, when you are out on your teaching practice, you will not be seeing your tutor as frequently. However, you should have at least one weekly meeting with your mentor to discuss progress and set targets. The QTS Standards should form the basis of this meeting and you should refer to the evidence collected so far to enable you to target set strengths, areas for developments and opportunities for the identification of new evidence.

Some people prefer to collect and evidence their Standards electronically; others will do this as a physical folder divided into sections according to the Standards and store the evidence in there. The method of collection needs to be agreed between you, your mentor and your tutor. As someone who reviews these documents regularly, personally I prefer a clearly organized file where I can follow the trail of collection with as much ease as possible.

The number of times the evidence has to be collected and the nature of the evidence will vary. However, it is reasonable to assume that you will have to provide a minimum of three pieces of evidence as proof that you are meeting the standards on a consistent basis. This is an important thing to note. You do not provide evidence three times and then never have to do this again. For example, Standard Q24 says that you must provide evidence to support the following statement:

> plan homework or other out-of-class work to sustain learners' progress and to extend and consolidate their learning.

You will need to provide the evidence, but this should become an embedded part of your practice as a teacher.

It is also reasonable to assume that the quality of the evidence you gather will improve as you go through your practice. Referring back to the homework example, the style and content of your homework will alter as your placements progress. You may want to reflect this in your file by collecting examples which show alternative ways you have required students to provide homework. For example, one homework may be a simple, individual fact-finding exercise or completion of a piece of work, whereas a second example may be one where you have required students to work as a group to produce a solution to a task set by you. Your evidence may also demonstrate that you have required your students to present solutions in different media: a piece of written text for one homework task; a picture for another; a long project or video diary for a third. You will also be asking your mentor to sign off that you have met this Standard fully. It would therefore be reasonable to expect that this evidence should come from the school that they are teaching at.

Task 5.1

Looking at the following Standard: how would you evidence that you have met the Standard?

Q24 Plan homework or other out-of-class work to sustain learners' progress and to extend and consolidate their learning.

This is considered to be one of the easier standards to evidence. Normally, a trainee would include, as evidence, examples of work set as homework as well as examples of the marked homework, showing clear evidence of effective assessment. You may also want to include details of out-of-school sessions or fixtures which you have organized. You may be able to use the same piece of work to evidence other Standards, for example, if the homework task that you are using for evidence includes any assessment, you may also use it to evidence Q12, which states the trainee should:

Know a range of approaches to assessment, including the importance of formative assessment.

Some of the Standards are more difficult to evidence. Standard Q13 often causes some difficulty:

Q13 Know how to use local and national statistical information to evaluate the effectiveness of their teaching, to monitor the progress of those they teach and to raise levels of attainment.

The issue here is what constitutes local and national statistical information as well as how you can use this to see how effective you are. A good solution for this would be to look at the levels at which a child is performing in your subject, at their target level and what the national expectations are for that particular student or group of students. Your effectiveness would be demonstrated if the students in your care managed to meet or exceed those levels. The evidence could therefore be the identification of the levels at the start and the end of your practice as well as what you have done to enable that process to happen, which may be details of the work set, examples of students' work and the results of your own formative assessment.

In some cases, there may be some confusion over how to display evidence that you are reaching some Standards in the Professional Attributes section, Standards 1–9. For example, Standard Q2 states that you must

Demonstrate the positive values, attitudes and behaviour they expect from children and young people.

This is clearly about how you present yourself in the classroom. It is about your values, behaviour and attitude, not the students. The evidence for this may be a witness statement from your tutor about how you generally conduct yourself or it may be noted in a classroom observation.

Further confusion can arise with Framework Standard Q3 which states that a trainee must:

(a) Be aware of the professional duties of teachers and the statutory framework within which they work.
(b) Be aware of the policies and practices of the workplace and share in collective responsibility for their implementation.

I have seen a number of files which simply include documents handed out at induction or downloaded from the school's network. This is not enough as it simply displays the ability to find a document and file it! It is not about the document, it is about how you use it in your practice. So, for example, if you download a behaviour policy document, you will then need to identify how you have used it. Highlight the piece of behaviour policy you have used and then demonstrate how you have implemented it. It is about your practice, so you need to show what you have done.

Using the same evidence to reference more than one Standard

The issue with homework and assessment raises a question frequently asked by trainees. Can they use the same piece of evidence for more than one Standard? The simple answer is yes. Many mentors and university tutors will, for example, provide a trainee with written feedback stating which Standards were evidence in that lesson. Consequently, the feedback may have five or more Standards on it, all of which can be used. Therefore, you can use this same evidence in a range of locations. How this is presented could be as a cross-reference, although some may prefer to have copies of the feedback placed in each section where it is relevant.

The QTS tests

As part of the Standards, you will be expected to complete three online tests in numeracy, literacy, and ICT (Q16). These have to be taken at an accredited centre and you will have to book tests in advance. The reason for the tests is that there is a minimum requirement of Standard which all must reach. It is not sensible to expect a trainee to produce evidence that they can use ICT in their own practice (Q17) and to enable students to use in their classrooms (Q23), if they do not have an appropriate level of understanding themselves. Also, as a teacher you will be writing in books and on boards, interactive or not, as well as communicating with the student's home, so again a good standard of English is essential. For each test, there are practice tests available online to give you an idea of how the tests are laid out and the sorts of questions that you will be asked.

Your university will inform you of where your nearest test centre is. However, it is realistic to expect that you may be away from your university on teaching practice. For example, you may be based at Sheffield Hallam University but your placement may be in York. Consequently, you may want to take a test close to your placement. The place to check for the availability of test centres and to book your tests is the TDA website who will have up-to-date records: http://www.tda.gov.uk/skillstests.aspx.

The one thing that you must not do is to put off the tests until the last moment! There will be lots of trainees trying to take the tests and a limited number of slots. It may also take you more than one attempt to take the test successfully so, as with everything, build in a contingency plan for such an eventuality. My strongest advice would be to book and take the tests as early as you possibly can to get them out of the way so that it is one hurdle overcome. If you put off the tests, you may run out of time and you must pass these tests to achieve your QTS. In my time, I have had to deal with a number of stressed students who have put the tests off and then struggled to pass.

The important thing is to identify your nearest test centre, book the test as early as you can and get help from the university if you are struggling to pass. Remember, although you can take the test as many times as is needed, you will have a limited time span to take it. Check with your university to make sure you know when the final date is for you to take your test. Do not get caught out!

Summary

After reading this chapter, you should now have a better understanding of what the QTS Standards are and how you need to evidence them. It should also be clear that you have a proactive role to play in the identification of opportunities to gather evidence. You will understand that the same piece of evidence can be used for a number of different Standards. It will also be clear that the key to success with gathering quality evidence is that you need to be organized in collecting and storing the evidence and that you should always be looking for opportunities to improve the evidence which you have. Remember, leave nothing to the last moment and work closely with your mentor.

Further reading

Denby, N. (2008) *How to Achieve Your QTS: A Guide for Students*. London: Sage.

6 | Time management

Contents

- What is time management?
- Why is time management important?
- Improving your time management
- Time management at school
- Marking and preparation
- Being realistic or 'Just say no!'
- Organizing your day
- Juggling school and university work
- Your work–life balance
- Summary
- Further reading

Learning objectives

In this chapter we look at the importance of:

- Effective time management and the trainee teacher
- Getting the balance right between school, university and home life.

QTS Standards

This chapter is particularly relevant to Q Standards 2, 3 and 6.

Relationships with children and young people

Q2 Demonstrate the positive values, attitudes and behaviour they expect from children and young people.

Frameworks

Q3 (a) Be aware of the professional duties of teachers and the statutory framework within which they work.

Q3 (b) Be aware of the policies and practices of the workplace and share in collective responsibility for their implementation.

Communicating and working with others

Q6 Have a commitment to collaboration and co-operative working.

What is time management?

Time management is exactly what it says – the management of time, or more precisely and importantly, your time. As we will see in this chapter, it is particularly important to you as a trainee teacher because you are also managing the time of your pupils, which makes it a little more complicated than just managing yourself. For some people, especially more mature students, time management is part of their everyday lives. They know that at 3:30 their children leave school so they have to organize for their care. If you have had a job which started at 9:00, you will have had to organize your time to make sure that you are out of bed, washed, fed, ready for the day before you head off for work and you have 50 minutes to do it in. You may have had to make sure that you catch the 07:30 bus because if you get the 07:45, you will be late for work. I could go on, but the point is already made. The importance of time management for the teacher is that they have to get it right because of the implications to the other people who are dependent on your attendance and punctuality.

If you are doing your teacher training straight from another university course or even school, then you will have become used to a certain amount of freedom which you will suddenly lose. You will have been used to being responsible for yourself, for turning up to lectures on time – even if your social life altered your attendance patterns from time to time! You may have had to do some group work and you may have had to meet some deadlines. But basically you have been responsible mainly for yourself and the clock is not the great dictator of your life. This is about to change and some do find the shock considerable.

When discussing with PGCE students what advice they would give to fellow trainees who were about to start the course, one comment stuck out as particularly relevant to this chapter:

> Be as prepared as possible. Get on top and keep on top
>   (Omar S, PGCE student, March 2010)

Why is time management important?

Basically, time management is important to you because you are responsible for the education of lots of other people. Your colleagues will be depending upon you too. You have the responsibility of a whole class to teach, so you have to be there – before the students and not after them – well prepared and ready to deliver an active and stimulating lesson every time.

If you get this wrong, then you will be seen as unreliable and unprofessional and, as indicated earlier in this book, Professional Attributes (which includes timekeeping) is a whole section of the Q Standards. It is this area where mentors are given their first impression of you as a trainee. It is simply something that you must get right instantly.

Your time is now so valuable that, if you get it wrong, the knock-on implications for other things becomes increasingly important. For example, if you put off your academic work in favour of your social life, your leisure time activity will be somewhat short-lived because you will have less time for the assignment, it will come into conflict with school work and you will finish up doing a poor job of both. This will then add to your stress levels, which may result in you being argumentative and falling out with your partner, for example. It is all about getting the balance right and allocating appropriate time to tasks.

Improving your time management

This is not as simple as buying a watch and getting a diary and making sure you write things down in your diary, although that would be a very good start. It is more about changing the way you look at your life. As indicated earlier, you are no longer simply responsible for yourself, you are responsible to others and have chosen to be so. If we add to this the complexities of your personal life, then it becomes even more important. You may, for example, have a family and time needs to be put aside purely for them or you may have other outside interests which require time. I will look at getting the balance right later on in this chapter, but first I will look at improving your time management within your working school life.

The first thing to remember is that you are a trainee, not a fully fledged teacher. Consequently your timetable will be relatively light, although it may not feel like it at first. You do have more time to play with and, especially in the early parts of your practice, mentors and other colleagues will not be expecting anything like the finished article, so you do have some breathing space. You have time within your day to prepare for lessons and to mark books. Make the most of it! Do not sit in the staffroom drinking tea all day, not only is it unhealthy but you are just putting off what needs to be done.

Time management at school

Let's look at the big picture first. You need time to get ready for school, travel to school, teach during the school day, prepare and mark work. You will also need to build in some time for any extra-curricular activities which you get involved in. So how much time do you need?

From the point of finding out where your first teaching practice is, you should be looking at how long you will need to make sure you are there on time, alert and ready to teach. So find out how far it is in terms of time to get from where you live to school to make sure you are there for morning briefing (never be late for this!). If you are on public transport, make sure that it gets you there early, not just on time, so make allowances for the bus being late. If you are driving, add an extra ten minutes as a contingency, as there may be delays and you do not want to turn up stressed before the day starts. Time pressure is a great source of stress in itself, so it is better give yourself more time and reduce some of that stress.

Now you have worked out your time for travel, work out how long (realistically) it takes you to get ready in the morning. You may find that you do not have the luxury of watching early morning TV any more – sorry! How long does it take for breakfast? Add this to your time and then you will be able to set the alarm for when you need to get up to get ready and get to work without the stress. Obviously, if you have a family to look after, then there will be their needs to be considered and these will have to be factored in.

The school day is very regimented. It is run according to timetables and you are part of that. You will know, or be able to find out, when the day starts and ends, when break and lunch are and when the different teaching periods of the day are. Get hold of your timetable as soon as you possibly can. Make sure you know the locations of the rooms and when the lesson starts. Do not sit in the staff resource centre until the bell goes before you start to move. Make sure you leave in good time to get to the room, with all the resources you need, before the bell sounds. You have to be there before the students at all times. If there is a delay, then this must be kept to a minimum as the start of the lesson sets the tone for the rest of it.

Another recommendation would be not to leave the school grounds if at all possible. If you go off-site at lunchtime, for example, make sure that you have plenty of time to get back. You cannot be late. At the end of the day, there may be a meeting which you have to attend. Make sure that you write this and any other appointment in your diary and stick to it. Normally, you can expect that the school day ends about one and half hours after the pupils have left. Do not think that your day ends when their day does, that is simply not the case!

Marking and preparation

The way you allocate time to this is up to you. However, my advice would be to use your free time as much as possible and use time at the end of the day. Try to reduce the amount of time you have to put into your school work at home to a minimum. You will not eradicate it completely but you can be in control of it and the more control you have, the more time you have for you.

When you first start teaching, you can expect to spend at least two hours preparation for each hour of delivery, sometimes more. There is also a good chance that you will need to develop appropriate resources for the sessions, which may be worksheets, video clips, sound bites. All this takes time. Your mentor may also want to see your lesson plans up to a week before you deliver the sessions, so this is not something that can be left to the last minute. You are responsible for the teaching and learning of the students in your charge and this is a serious profession. So make sure that you factor enough time in to do this. Time for preparation is one of the most common grumbles of teachers. However, you do have this built into your timetable to allow for this, so use it wisely.

You may be able to claw some time back by looking at other, similar resources from a variety of sources. The internet is an obvious starting place with a range of sites available to you which can act as resource exchanges. You should not, however, under any circumstances, take a lesson plan from a website and try to use it wholesale with classes which you are teaching. You must adapt to the needs of the class you are teaching but it could give you some very good ideas to base your new lesson on. Whatever your situation, there is a good chance that someone has delivered a similar lesson before and is happy to share this with you.

Marking is another area which will take up a great deal of your time and it is no longer enough to take books in, add a tick and hand them back. Marking needs to be done and done well. The time which you take to mark will depend on the nature and size of task which you have given to the class. However, it is important to be strict with yourself and say that you will mark the work as soon as it is handed in and returned to the students as soon as possible. Marking work is a great responsibility. It is not simply to do with assessment, it is also about recognizing that the work that a student does is important to you as a teacher. If you do not take your marking seriously, then why should your students take you and your lessons seriously?

Whenever possible, make sure that you not only grade the work but explain why the mark was given and, more importantly, how to get to the next level. The importance of this formative assessment should not be underestimated; writing 'good work' is not good enough on your part. By telling the student how they can reach the next level sets the bar again. It also indicates that you believe that they can achieve the new target. It is a very positive as well as informative thing to do. (I will look at the whole issue of assessment for learning in a separate chapter.) Do not do the marking in front of the TV with a glass of wine, however tempting that may be, save that as your reward for completion. You need to find the best location which you can get to perform this task and the least chance of disturbance.

Task 6.1

Think about what your most productive working environment is.

What resources do you need?

Have you identified a place where you can work?

Have you ensured that you will be able to concentrate on the task?

Are there any other demands on your time at the moment?

Being realistic or 'Just say no!'

This is one area which many trainees struggle with. Someone asks you to do something for them, which is not included in your timetable. What should you do? Not only are you unable to say how long particular tasks may take, but you may also be willing to take on tasks because you feel you have to or that you should do. Many people feel they are unable to say no to requests, even if they know they do not have the time to do it. Some staff may unreasonably put pressure on you to perform tasks which they do not want to do. Although I have said that building good working relationships is important, it does not make you a doormat.

Organizing your day

I hope that I have managed to instil the importance of organization within this chapter and how it fits into the whole issue of balance and time management. Therefore, the next action must be to work out just how much time you have in your day – you will need the timetable from school to do this. Set out your day in hour blocks from midnight to midnight in Task 6.2. You may also choose to use different colours for different activities.

Juggling school and university work

This is a problem for a great many trainees and it is also something which creates some confusion as to your role. Are you a teacher or are you a student? I would suggest that this changes as your professional practice develops; it is a spectrum along which you will progress. At the start, you are clearly a student but the further you get into your course, the closer and closer you get to being a teacher. Eventually, there is a tipping point when you move from the student to the teacher. This is usually also the point when trainees stop asking why they are doing their university work or assignments and understand the links between their own development and the work set. However, this is not to say that this issue is not a very real one which many struggle with.

The weighting for the successful completion of the course usually depends more upon the completion of the university work than your skills as a classroom teacher as evidenced by meeting the QTS Standards. Some may see this as unfair and weighted towards those trainees who are better with the theory than the practice. This may be a reasonable argument. However, it is important to remember that you have to pass all sections of the course and word gets around much quicker of a strong practitioner in the classroom than one who can simply write about it. The ideal scenario is someone who is knowledgeable about the theory but who can also put this into effective practice in the classroom. You need to know about different learning theories and styles, what the legal aspects of teaching are, what the research says about teaching and learning and how to effectively engage with virtual learning environments (VLEs), for example. It may not help that you have a mentor who sees the school work as more important than the university work. Either way, it is there and must be tackled.

The first thing to note is that you are given the time to do the university work courtesy of a light timetable. The second important fact is that you will know well in advance what the dates are for the submission of university work. You will also know the titles of the assignments and may well also have access to a list of recommended readings which will help you to complete your assignments. Consequently, it is back to our old friend, organization and time management. If you start your assignments late, you may come into conflict with teaching assessment deadlines and then you have the problem of identifying your priority. Depending on the nature of the assignment, you may need to collect and analyse data and you could leave yourself in a tight corner if, for some reason, you fail to collect it. Leaving it too late could result in handling in substandard work which may need resubmitting. If this is your final/professional year, failing a piece of coursework could result in a job offer being retracted or even you failing the course. It is simply not worth gambling with this. It is also better to do little and often than try to do it all in a couple of days.

The advice is, therefore, to start the assignments as soon as is feasible and make sure that you keep at it. It is easy to put them on the back boiler when you are in school and the university seems like a different world, but avoid doing this. Be sure you know the assessment criteria for the assignment and make sure that you hit them. Many assignments will allow you to chunk the work you have into sections – take advantage of this. You may wish to set specific times aside for university work (something which I would recommend) and others for school work. I would also recommend that you set yourself a timeline for your work and make sure that you hit the key targets by the dates specified. Also, build in some slippage time to give you the chance to look at your work and revise parts which you may not be happy with. If you do this, I guarantee that the quality of the work will be higher and your stress levels will be lower.

Your work–life balance

A great deal is said about the work–life balance. Everyone seems to be keen on it until there are pressured deadlines at work and then the balance would seem to move towards work and away from life. Everything I have said so far on this chapter seems to revolve around organization and the effective use of your time, which is reasonable. However, the stress has been towards work at the moment and little given to you as the person. Everyone's situation is different of course. Some may be single; others may be in relationships and/or married. Some may have children of varying ages and some may have care issues which have to be taken into consideration. Whatever your situation, there has to be time for you in there somewhere otherwise you will simply not function well as a teacher. Recharging batteries is very important.

Wherever possible, leave school behind you at some part of the day – although not when you are teaching! If you have a family, it is important that you spend good quality time with them, they are, after all, your support when time gets difficult and it is unreasonable to expect them to take a backseat to your classes all the time. If you take this approach, they will be much more supportive on those occasions when you need to spend more time than you should on school work. I know of teachers who have become so engrossed in their school work that they have not noticed the gulf growing between those and the ones they love. It is important to avoid this.

Now, I am not advocating that a younger trainee with no responsibility should unwind in a club or pub until the early hours – there is a time and a place for this and with a Y9 class at 8:50 the following day this is not it. However, you have to unwind at some time. How you do this is up to you. You may have a hobby which you follow. You may climb, you may go to the cinema, you may help with the local Guides or grow super-sized onions. In many ways, it does not matter. What does matter is that you have time for you and that work does not take over your life and become a source of frustration and resentment as well as a possible threat to your health.

Task 6.2

Identify what you **HAVE** to do in that day (this is where the timetable comes in). Identify what other tasks you have to do – this may include getting dressed and eating before you go to school, travel to and from school, etc. Always make sure you build in some flexibility to this task – some days it may take longer to prepare for school – better to say it takes 45 minutes than 30 if you take 35.

Identify timeslots which are not allocated – this is potential free time.

A possible example has been given on the next page.

Time (From Midnight)	Activity	Note
12:00	Sleep	
1:00	Sleep	
2:00	Sleep	
3:00	Sleep	
4:00	Sleep	
5:00	Sleep	
6:00	Sleep	get up for school 6:30
7:00	eat and leave	leave for school 7:45
8:00		
9:00		
10:00		
11:00		
12:00		
1:00		
2:00		
3:00		
4:00		
5:00		
6:00		
7:00		
8:00		
9:00		
10:00		
11:00	Sleep	

As you can see from this exercise, you do not have as much flexible time as you may think. Consequently, you must be realistic about what you can take on. The golden rule is not to take on more than you can do and, in your case, doing this very well is important. The implications of doing things poorly, or not at all, can result in important tasks which impact on others not being done well and your image in the department being severely damaged. It may also mean that you do not perform at your best, knowing that you have taken on something you cannot do and worrying about it. It is much better to be in a position where you are realistic and say no when you know that you cannot do what is asked of you.

Summary

In this chapter we have looked at the issues surrounding time management, including how to improve your time management and juggling your university and school life. We have also looked at issues of work–life balance and what happens if we get it wrong. Having read this chapter, you should also have a greater understanding of the importance of your personal organization as well the importance of being realistic about what you take on.

Further reading

Adair, J. and Allen, M. (1999) *Time Management and Personal Development.* London: Thorogood.

Bird, P. (2008) *Time Management.* London: Hodder.

Clegg, B. (1999) *Instant Time Management.* London: Kogan Page.

Forsyth, P. (2007) *Successful Time Management.* London: Kogan Page.

7 | **Reflective practice**

Contents

- What is reflective practice?
- The importance of reflective practice
- Reflection as a learning tool
- Reflection in action
- Reflective partners
- Critical reflection
- Summary
- Further reading

Learning objective

In this chapter, we look at reflective practice and how it impacts on your ability to develop as a teacher and an individual.

QTS Standards

This chapter is particularly relevant to Standards 7, 8 and 9.

Personal and professional development

Q7 (a) Reflect on and improve their practice, and take responsibility for identifying and meeting their developing professional needs.

(b) Identify priorities for their early professional development in the context of induction.

Q8 Have a creative and constructively critical approach towards innovation, being prepared to adapt their practice where benefits and improvements are identified.

Q9 Act upon advice and feedback and be open to coaching and mentoring.

What is reflective practice?

The first thing that we need to think about is exactly what we mean by reflection. In a nutshell, reflection is the way in which we look at ourselves. We look at ourselves in a number of ways all of the time. As a basic, physical approach, we look at ourselves to check what we look like – we want to look and feel good and we want others to think that too. We may well ask for external verification of our opinion, for example, asking 'Do I look alright?', hoping of course that the answer will be the one that you want and not 'no'! You are inviting others to give feedback on you.

Obviously, while we can draw parallels with this scenario, being reflective in our practice is not looking at the way you physically appear to others, although it may have an impact upon it. Reflective practice means taking an honest look at yourself and your actions and asking questions such as 'How well did that go?' or 'Could I have done that better?' You may well invite others into this process by asking their opinion on how something went. You may, for example, be having difficulty with a class or situation and so ask someone to observe you to solicit their opinion. We will call this person your reflective partner, someone who is willing to support you by being critical of your performance in the classroom. I will look at the role of the critical friend later in this chapter.

The importance of reflective practice

The ability to reflect upon your own practice is critical to your success as a teacher. Effective learning will not occur unless you reflect. Standard Q7(a) states that you must clearly and continually evidence that you do the following:

(a) Reflect on and improve their practice, and take responsibility for identifying and meeting their developing professional needs.

Learning through your school experiences is equally, if not more, important than the theoretical knowledge which you will gain from your university lessons. As a trainee teacher, you are encouraged to actively reflect upon your performance in the classroom all the time. You start this by the feedback which you are expected to do at the end of each lesson you teach. In this feedback, you will look at how the lesson went, what went well and which areas need improvement. Some trainees see this as an inconvenience, taking up too much time and simply another hoop that you have to jump through. However, that underestimates the importance of the activity and, in some ways, is arrogant in that you are effectively saying, 'I am fine' and 'I do not need to improve'. Basically, you are at the start of your teaching practice and you need all the help you can get, even if it is from yourself!

You also need to feel comfortable about doing this. You need to ask yourself if you have the ability to be self-critical. Some people cannot accept that they may make mistakes and need to improve, and so self-evaluation and reflective practice are a difficult task for them. Some people are overly critical of themselves. Such people are open to reflection but sometimes have difficulty in accepting that they can improve. Clearly the ideal is to be somewhere in the middle: able to accept criticism and identify ways to improve, and then put it into action.

One thing which I have always encouraged trainees to do is to have their own reflective journal. There are many ways to do this. You could have an online blog, for example. You may, like me, have an old-fashioned paper journal which I write in every night. As I consider this to be an important activity, which I enjoy, I have an A5-sized soft leather diary in which I write down my reflections of the day. I do this using a green fountain pen because it makes me feel good, simple as that. But why do it at all? Surely I have been teaching for too long to carry on doing this? Not at all! I reflect on any number of things: from how sessions went, how I reacted in meetings, how I felt when someone challenged me, what made me smile during the day. It helps me to step back and take another look at things to see how I could have improved upon situations through the day. This type of journal can also be good for you as a trainee teacher as it will allow you to see your teaching practice from a wider perspective. To do this even more effectively, the reflective journal should include your thoughts about how others perceive a situation, why they reacted in the way they did, how they feel and what you have done to influence things. You may wish to divide your reflection into different sections, those which are emotional and those which are not, although sometimes one will impact on the other.

On the whole, what we are trying to establish is a good level of self-awareness and insight, to take forward the good things and do something about those areas which you feel need improvement. No one can force you to do this, it's up to you, but the more open you are to it, the more effective you will become at it and the less likely you will be at jumping into situations without thinking about the consequences.

Reflection as a learning tool

In many ways you are reflecting in life all the time, dealing with situations by remembering how a similar situation turned out before and building upon that experience. If you burnt yourself lighting a fire, then you will be more careful next time, i.e. you will have reflected upon what you have done and learnt from it. Clearly this is something of an extreme example but the point is made. We do something, we reflect on it, and based on that reflection, we either repeat that action or change it to a more appropriate one.

Obviously, you will be mainly concerned with reflection in teaching but it is important to remember that teaching is much more than standing in front of a class and that the human interaction issue is equally important. You may have to reflect on your interpersonal skills much more than you may have done before. In your capacity as a trainee teacher you will be looking to apply the theory that you have learnt in university lessons in 'live' situations. You may have undertaken some role play but, unless you are lucky and your university has some arrangements with local schools, you will have not have come into direct contact with school children until you are in the classroom. You will also learn in a different way in university to learning in school placements. You will be applying what you have learnt in university to real-life situations with impressionable young people. Getting it wrong can cause problems for both you and your students. You do not have the luxury of time and the safety of the academic situation that you have when you are in university. You have to respond there and then and the fact that students are adding unknown factors into your well-planned lessons can confuse what you intended to deliver.

When you are first on placement and, more importantly, when you are first in front of a class, it can all seem somewhat frantic and confusing at times and you will wonder where the time goes. However, you will have a reduced timetable, you will not have the responsibilities of a qualified teacher and you have the luxury of being a trainee. So you will not be expected to get it right first time, in fact, you will be expected to make mistakes. However, your university will be encouraging you to reflect upon your practice and the QTS Standards demand that you show evidence that you do this. According to Standard Q7(a), trainees should:

> Reflect on and improve their practice, and take responsibility for identify-ing and meeting their developing professional needs.

As a professional, you will be expected to reflect upon your actions all the time. You will be responsible for the well-being and development of your students. It is a huge responsibility and one which should not be taken lightly. As you gain more experience to bolster your knowledge, you will become a more confident and competent teacher. Reflection, as identified in Q7, is therefore a key part of your own learning and development.

As professionals, we must reflect all the time, not only in our classroom practice, but also in our relationships with others. A professional should think before they speak and not just leap in. Such people have developed effective tact. Some people appear to be naturally more tactful than others, whereas some react first and think later. I would encourage you to develop skills of tact, you must think before you react.

Task 7.1

Think about what would happen if you simply responded without thought, what would the impact be of your actions? How could this impact on your job, your career and your relationships, both in the classroom and the staffroom?

Regardless of the situation, you will be going through the same process of the reflective cycle. The process has been discussed by many academics and the same basic model applies, with the one illustrated in Figure 7.1 by Gibbs as good as any.

As we can see from this model, there is no end to the process because different factors can come into the situation as each situation is unique, especially in the teaching profession where we are dealing with a range of individuals from Y7 students to local authority (LA) officials and the way we think things should turn out may not do so.

Figure 7.1 The reflective cycle
Source: Gibbs (1988)

As we can see from the model, reflection is a cyclical event, starting with the event itself, through analysis and moving towards an action plan to identify what you would do if the situation arose again. You may question, with some justification, why you should reflect if every situation is unique due to the characters involved, i.e. can the same situation ever happen again? Well, the answer is that another situation may be very similar and, with increasing experience, you will be able to understand what may happen and be prepared for it. In essence, you start to anticipate what may happen in certain situations and the more experienced you become, the better at this you become. As a young man in my mid-teens playing rugby against teams who had what I thought to be 'old men' playing for them, I was confident that I would always be able to outrun them but they always seemed to know where I would be and get there before me. When I got to the end of my playing life, I found that I had turned into that old man myself as a result of experience – it's all a big circle!

It's the same with your lessons. You deliver it; you reflect upon its effectiveness – what went right and what went wrong – and then see if you can reduce the wrong parts by trying new techniques; talking the issue through with others; but reflecting and analysing all the time to enable you to become an increasingly effective teaching professional. It is therefore clear that reflection, where you are honest about your successes and failures, is a powerful learning tool for you and you should embrace it wholeheartedly. You can make your reflection even more effective by moving the process forward to critical analysis and employing the use of a reflective partner. We will discuss these issues later in the chapter.

Generally, I have wanted to avoid referencing academic works in this book but in this section I feel that I must do so as it helps to emphasize the points that will be made. To look at reflection as a one-dimensional activity may not be realistic. Reflection does, to some extent, indicate that you need the luxury of time to enable you to gather all your thoughts before you move forward in some future time. This may not be practical and I feel that we may need to distil the concept to allow for this. Schön (1987), for example, states that reflection can be divided into two sections: *reflection in action,* where you think on your feet, and *reflection on action,* where you are retrospective, thinking the situation through. So far in this chapter, I think that we have been considering what Schön would refer to as reflection on action, rather than reflection in action and it is this which I intend to look at now.

Reflection in action

Remember the old rugby player, being just where I did not want him to be all the time? I feel that he was a prime example of reflection in action, thinking on his feet, basing his action on his experience of previous events, something which can be done with increasing effectiveness if you know the individuals who may be involved, because your experience tells you what they are likely to do in certain situations. It's not just having the experience; it's the learning from that experience which is the key thing.

We see this in schools too. There are certain teachers who seem to know exactly what to do, how to calm a situation down in the event of conflict, how to motivate students whom we could get nothing out of, how to rescue a lesson which has gone totally wrong because of a lack of resources or failure of hardware in all its forms or descriptions. I have stood in wonder looking at these individuals until I found eventually that others were looking at me in the same way as I gained that experience myself.

The ability to access reflection in action is not something which can be undertaken without a considerable amount of reflection on action. You cannot simply leap into a situation and hope for the best. Reflection in action has arisen from being in the situation many times before, from talking to colleagues about the situation, getting their ideas and thoughts, finding out what may have influenced those situations and what could be done the next time. This is as true in the classroom as the playground.

The difference between reflection in action and reflection on action is the input of experience and knowledge. The more you experience a situation, the more you are aware of possible solutions to it. If you add the further ingredient of knowledge, which may be of the way an individual is likely to react, the procedures in place to deal with a particular situation, or simply being secure in your 'Plan B', then you are likely to be on solid ground. As a consequence of this, you may find that you respond quickly, almost without thinking, to a situation and that the reflection on the situation comes later on, when you have the luxury of time to think on it, to move towards the reflection on action. As a trainee, you may find that your reflection in action is somewhat lacking due to inexperience and uncertainty, but this will change with experience. Do not think that the more experienced teachers ever dispense with reflection on action, they do not. They face new situations every day which they will reflect upon, things which have worked with class x before will suddenly not, so they reflect upon this and then act.

Task 7.2

Think of a situation where you practise reflection in action. How does this make you feel? Can you remember a time when you could not do this? How did you feel? What is the difference between the you now and the you then?

Reflective partners

As indicated earlier, I feel that you can only go so far with reflection if you do this by yourself. True, you can do it in isolation, but the process is much better and more productive if you have a reflective partner who will work with you. The role of the reflective partner is not to tell you what to do. They may offer opinions, they may be totally honest in what they say, they may offer advice, but they are not there to give you all the answers, indeed, they may not have the answers themselves.

Choosing a reflective partner

The role of the reflective partner is a very important one and one which holds a considerable amount of responsibility. I also feel that to ask someone to be a reflective partner is something of an honour, as it shows that you trust and respect them enough to work with you to help you to improve your practice. So who do you ask? This is always the difficult part. As we are in teaching, I would advocate a fellow teacher. While I feel that the use of a reflective partner outside the profession has its advantages and can bring fresh ideas to situations, someone who understands the training profession would probably be the best option.

If we accept that someone within the teaching profession would be a good option, we then need to take the step one move further and look to who we can select. I would suggest that you refine further and select a reflective partner within the school that you teach in. This is because that person will have an insight into how the school in which you work functions, knows the players within the classroom, and knows the key relationships.

Further on from this, it should be someone you can trust, can open up to and will be honest with you without being judgemental. I would also opt for someone who is experienced within the teaching profession rather than a fellow trainee who may have the same issues as you. You may choose to have someone in your department or you may choose to work with someone who is outside the department to give a slightly different perspective on issues than you may get from your mentor, for example.

You should also be clear about what you want to get from the experience. Your reflective partner is not there to tell you that everything you do is right. For example, they must be in a position to point out issues as they see them, to offer advice rather than solutions and feel that they can be honest with you, safe in the knowledge that you will not take offence.

Task 7.3

Think about the sort of person you would want as a reflective partner.

Identify someone who you think would be a good partner.

Think about how you could ask this person to be your reflective partner.

Setting the ground rules

Let us assume that you have identified a reflective partner and that they have agreed. As this activity can, at times, be very personal, you may find it a good idea to establish some ground rules which you will stick to when meeting. I will not tell you what these should be because it is your choice how you operate this relationship but here are some pointers which you may consider:

- *Confidentiality* – you may be discussing particular students or other individuals so it may be important that you both exercise confidentiality in this area.

- *No ideas are bad ideas* – if people think that they cannot be open and honest, they may not volunteer points which may be beneficial.

- *Equality of status* – if you feel that you are not of equal status within this relationship, then you may not feel comfortable to share your concerns.

- *Space to think* – you may both feel that you need space to think about issues and return to them at a later time or date when you have had time to reflect.

- *Honesty* – some may leave this out, or not even think about it, but it is important that both parties are honest with each other.

- *Time and location* – you may want to agree a weekly time and location for this activity, so that it becomes part of the routine.

These are just a few ideas to get you thinking about what you may want for your ground rules. It is up to you and your reflective partner what they are but it is important that you both buy into this process and adhere to it.

Task 7.4

Identify six proposed ground rules which you would be happy to have when working with your reflective partner.

Critical reflection

Critical reflection differs from what could be referred to as normal reflection by the level to which you do it. Critical reflection tends to take into account a wider view. We may, for example, not only look at how we responded to a particular situation, but expand it into what it is about ourselves which made us react in this way, what our own experiences are which may have influenced our response. We may then look at the situation again and challenge the way we dealt with it, or challenge the way that society says that we should do it. If we are conforming to a social norm of expectation, we may start to think about the values behind it and question if they are right. In school, for example, there may be cultural issues which you have taken for granted and not challenged. One of the issues of reflection is that, if you do not document it, and the situation only comes up rarely, you may well forget how you handled it and how you decided you could impact upon it.

At the start of this book, I encouraged you to produce a reflective journal, somewhere to write down the events of the day, how you felt, how you dealt with things, what the outcomes were. This is useful in itself in terms of recording your progress through the year and you will be surprised on how you have developed. It is also a very useful record of how you have handled situations and as a reflective tool, it is invaluable. The big advantage of the use of a journal is as an anchor point which you can refer back to. After all, there are a considerable number of situations which may be important at the time but may not occur again for a year or more. In this case, there is a good chance that you will not have the instant recall of how you dealt with this situation if it came up again, but wish you had. The solution you came up with the first time may not be the solution this time but it will give you a starting point and may well help you avoid making a situation worse.

Some would say that critical reflection is a sign of a continual progression towards maturity within the profession, that ability to almost step back from the situation and look at it from a wider context. I would agree with this as effective critical reflection will allow for the inclusion of the experience of the individual and not just a reaction to the here and now.

Writing up your reflection

The key thing to remember about the journal is that it is yours and yours alone. Do not feel that you have to share it with anyone. If you choose to do so that is up to you but be aware that you are not only laying yourself open to the opinions of others but that you may well restrict yourself in what you write in case others read it. If this is the case, then you cannot be fully open and honest with it. Here are a few tips about writing:

1. Make sure you make time to write in the journal, every day if possible. Make it part of your routine. If you do not, then you will soon get out of the habit and it will be a chore when you do sit down to it.

2. Select your own medium for writing. You may wish to write online, you may wish to write in a notebook. Choose whatever feels right for you. I, for example, write with a fountain pen, in a book which is somewhat battered but bound, and in green ink. I am not sure why, but it feels right to me, and I would not feel good writing with a ballpoint pen.

3. Do not worry about what you write or how you write it – you could even draw in it if you want, no one is going to mark it! It is important that you capture your feelings as well as what happened and how it was resolved, if at all. These feelings are important for the critical reflection you will do when you stand back from the situation and consider it later.

4. Confidentiality is important. Although I have said that this is for yourself and no one else, journals have found their way into the hands of others and some of the things you say could be considered negative or offensive to some. Avoid using real names.

5. Reflection is not just about those important, critical incidents. It is also about the everyday life you lead, the normal daily events, the things people say. Sometimes, looking back on the everyday helps us cope when we perceive times are difficult.

6. Write the answers to the tasks in the journal too so you can access them easily. They can help in your reflective practice.

Summary

In this chapter we have explored what we mean by reflection and its use as an educational tool for our own development. We have identified the difference between reflection and critical reflection as well as discussing the role of the reflective partner and how to work with them. I hope that, following this chapter, you will understand the importance of reflection within educational practice and take an active role in it.

Further reading

Dymoke, S. and Harrison, J. (2008) *Reflective Teaching and Learning: A Guide to Professional Issues for Beginning Secondary Teachers*. London: Sage.

Gibbs, G. (1988) *Learning by Doing: A Guide to Teaching and Learning Methods*. Clevedon: Further Education.

Schön, D.A (1987) *Educating the Reflective Practitioner*. San Francisco: Jossey-Bass.

8 Formative and summative reviews

Contents

- Putting the reviews into context
- Preparing for your review
- Handling feedback
- Action planning
- Summary
- Further reading

Learning objectives

By the end of this chapter you will be able to understand:

- The difference between formative and summative reviews
- Your role in preparing for the review
- How to use the feedback given at the reviews
- How to action plan effectively.

QTS Standards

This chapter is particularly relevant to Q Standards 7, 8 and 9.

Personal and professional development

Q7 (a) Reflect on and improve their practice, and take responsibility for identifying and meeting their developing professional needs.

(b) Identify priorities for their early professional development in the context of induction.

Q8 Have a creative and constructively critical approach towards innovation, being prepared to adapt their practice where benefits and improvements are identified.

Q9 Act upon advice and feedback and be open to coaching and mentoring.

Putting the reviews into context

The formative and summative reviews are key milestone checks on your progression as a trainee teacher. These will be used by your mentor to indicate to you exactly where you are in terms of progress in the classroom and the collection of your evidence towards QTS status. It will also be an opportunity for you to identify future targets, strengths and areas for development.

You will, on the whole, be measured against the QTS Standards and how well you have done in meeting them. It is important at this point to recognize that the standards do not change as your teaching experiences progress: Q1 remains the same for each of your practices. However, it is important to recognize that the expectations of your mentor will change the closer you get to completing your teacher training programme. Mentors will talk with each other about trainees and where they expect them to be within the practice. Comments such as 'OK for a first placement but will have to up their game on the next placement' are common. Such expectations are not necessarily explicitly laid out, rather they can be an implicit expectation. What may be acceptable on your first practice may not be on your second. Some trainees may reach a plateau in that they seem to have developed as far as they can and seem unable to take the next step forward. This is hard for some trainees to accept. I will look at these issues in Chapter 10 on failing your placement.

So the reviews are therefore milestones in your practice. The reviews should occur once about halfway through your teaching practice and a final summative report at the end of the teaching practice. In your final placement, the summative review will decide whether or not you have met all of the standards to allow you to achieve QTS status. Consequently, this final summative review is very important and should be handled appropriately.

The timescale for the reviews will be given by your university and the results of the summative reports will be taken to exam boards to allow them to decide if trainees are allowed to proceed to future teaching practice or not. In some cases, progression will be allowed but with strict targets and deadlines attached. But for the vast majority of trainees progression to the next stage of their training or career is automatic.

The content of the review should not be a surprise to you as you are being continually monitored by your mentor, colleagues and members of staff, all of whom will be talking to each other. You will have had observations, formal and informal meetings with your mentor and your own teaching experiences. You will have also been working on gathering evidence for your QTS file so you should know pretty much where you are. If you are an effective reflective practitioner, you should also be well aware of your strengths and weaknesses and you should be able to identify a great deal of them yourself. Consequently, you should be able to go to your review, formative or summative, knowing what to expect.

Preparing for your review

As this is a crucial part of your ongoing assessment, the preparation for the review should be handled in a professional and practical manner. You will have your time plan from your university, so you will know when your review is due to happen. Your mentor should also have a copy of this, however, they are busy people, so I would recommend that you remind your mentor well in advance as to when the review needs to take place and set a diary time for this meeting. Your mentor will also need time to prepare for this.

The layout of the review document will vary from institution to institution but the content will be pretty much the same. There will be a breakdown of each of the standards and your mentor will be required to state if these have been met or not; if they are an area of strength; if they are satisfactory; or if they are an area for development. The mentor will also be expected to give you an overall grade for that group of standards.

This being done, the mentor will then identify a number of targets as well as how you will be expected to evidence those targets together with a deadline. So, for example, you may be struggling to identify how you are meeting standard Q23: 'Design opportunities for learners to develop their literacy, numeracy and ICT skills.' If this is the case, then your mentor may set you a target of booking an ICT suite and developing resources to enable you to teach a group of effective lessons using technology.

There will also be an opportunity for the mentor to add general comments on your progress to date. On the summative assessment, the mentor will also be expected to produce a final report on your performance on the three areas of Professional Attributes, Professional Knowledge and Understanding, and Professional Skills. You will also be graded on this section. The comments on the summative report may also be a way of passing information to future mentors. For example, they may want to suggest that you need more experience with behaviour management at KS4 or that you have not had the opportunity to attend a parents evening.

So far, it would appear that you are a passive participant in this process. It is true that someone is making a professional judgement about you according to the evidence presented to them but surely that puts you in a strong position. If you know what the standards are and know how you are addressing them, you will be demonstrating to the mentor that you are active in your own development, that you are professional in your approach and, most importantly, that you are moving away from being a student towards being a teacher. In the Q Standards themselves, three of them (Q7, Q8 and Q9) are concerned with how you take responsibility for identifying your own professional needs. What better way than to be an active partner in your own assessment!

Task 8.1

Look at the QTS Standards and identify three areas where you feel that you could improve your practice. Identify real, achievable targets for yourself and how you intend to meet them.

Naturally, it is helpful if you turn up to your meeting prepared. You should have your QTS file with you (if your evidence is as a hard copy) and a number of targets which you have identified for yourself which you should discuss with your mentor. These are your targets, this is your career, *you* should take professional and personal responsibility for them. Your mentor's role is to help you to become a competent and qualified teacher. They will have themselves gone through this role and via their own continual professional development be used to setting their own targets. This will help them to identify targets which you may have missed or they may suggest that you provide stronger evidence in some areas. Whatever the situation, you will both have to sign the formative or summative feedback as an acknowledgement that the meeting has taken place and the resulting targets have been set.

Handling feedback

Many people approach feedback with some trepidation, seeing it as a negative experience. Before we go further into this issue, I think that it is important for you to note down how you feel about receiving feedback.

Task 8.2

Write down five things which you feel about receiving feedback.

1	
2	
3	
4	
5	

What is it in your own experience which makes you have these feelings?

As indicated, receiving feedback can be a stressful event. Giving it can also be difficult too, especially if the feedback is less than positive. One thing to reflect upon in this chapter is about how you give feedback to your own students. How can not only what you say but how you say it affect how they feel about themselves, their work and their relationship with you? If done well, everyone should come out of the experience seeing a clear way forward. If it is done poorly, it can lead to frustration, confusion and resentment.

During the course of your review meeting, you may have had targets set for you which you did not see coming. Your mentor may also have identified areas for development which you previously perceived as strengths. Your grading may not be as high as you have wanted it to be. All sorts of issues may have been identified for your continued progress. As this is a judgement on your professional development, many people take this very personally. However, it is important to extract yourself to some extent from this feedback and remember that it is your skills as a teacher, not you as a person which is the source of the scrutiny and one of the roles of the mentor is that of the honest, critical friend.

Giving feedback which may be perceived as negative is not an easy thing to do for a mentor especially if the mentor gets on well with the trainee. This is one reason why some mentors try to maintain a little distance from their trainee, just in case such a situation arises.

As indicated earlier, it is important to be realistic in your expectations and to be open about what is said within the meeting. I feel that, for example, it is unreasonable for a mentor to mark you very highly at the end of your first placement, especially if you are on a PGCE course. Most institutions use a scoring system similar to Ofsted, i.e., a 1 to 4 grading, with 1 being outstanding and 4 being below the expected standard. Do you honestly think that it is possible to score 1 and 2 on issues such as Professional Skills and Understanding after only a few weeks? How easy would that make training to be a teacher appear? It is much more realistic to expect and be happy with a grade 3 at an early stage, as you are only a new trainee at this point. Higher grades can be expected further into the course when you start to tip from student to teacher but then only if you earn them. It is also not unreasonable to get grade 3 in your final summative review. Wherever you are at the end of your final placement, you are only just starting as a teacher and, believe it or not, the demands of your NQT year and beyond will be much greater than the course you have been working on. The main priority during your placement is to avoid getting a grade 4. This is not to say that you should try for the minimum just to scrape through, as this would be a foolish strategy. We should all strive to be the best that we can but some will take longer than others to get there.

The most important thing to take from the meeting is the way forward. No matter how well you are doing, it would not be much of a review unless you could identify targets where you can improve and develop or areas where you are struggling. If you have heard things which you did not want to hear or face up to, taking your bat and ball home is not an option. There is a very good chance that you will be teaching shortly after your review so you need to remain focused on the job in hand. You are, after all, responsible for the education of the class in front of you at that time. You may, with further reflection, wish to return to your mentor for additional clarification of issues raised. This is fine, especially if there is an area for development which has been identified. You need to be clear in your mind what you have to do. Remember, this may not have been an easy experience for you and maybe not for your mentor either but making sure that the relationship remains positive and professional is your key to success.

So, you have had your review, you are clear about where exactly you stand in terms of strengths and areas for development and the level which you are currently functioning at. The next stage is to identify how you are going to improve: action planning.

Action planning

By action planning, I mean taking active control of the next steps. The better trainees will be active in planning their own development, the weaker ones may expect their mentors to do it for them. I strongly advise you to be the better trainee! As indicated in the last section, you should have come to the review with a good idea of your progress so far and some targets of your own which you should have discussed with your mentor.

The first thing to do is to make sure that you have identified and agreed with your mentor your development targets. Make sure you understand why these are your targets. Have a good understanding of this because they may impact on other areas of your teaching practice. The next thing to do is to identify how, exactly, you will provide evidence that you meet these targets. Make sure that this is not vague; it needs to be real and specific to what your target is. The final thing to do is to set yourself a deadline for when this target will be met. However, an important note is that meeting and evidencing this target once is not enough. The outcome from your target is part of an ongoing process, consequently, the target is not something to be met once and forgotten about, it's about embedding it into your practice. Whatever your plan, it will need to be agreed and signed by both you and your mentor.

If the plan relates to your formative review, you will be expected to meet the deadlines before your summative review. If your plan is on the back of the summative review, it should inform your practice for your next teaching practice or your NQT year. It is all about taking control of the situation and your own development and should be seen as an empowering opportunity.

Summary

In this chapter we have looked at the issue of formative and summative reviews, handling feedback and action planning. We have also looked at your responsibility in the process of identifying realistic targets and how you can use a better understanding of how you feel about feedback to inform the feedback that you give to your own students.

Further reading

Montgomery, D. (2005) *Helping Teachers Develop Through Classroom Observation.* London: David Fulton.
Wragg, E.C. (1998) *Introduction to Classroom Observation.* London: Routledge.

9 | **Visits and observations**

Contents

- Observing others teach
- Using the observations of others to guide your teaching
- Being observed
- Handling feedback
- Visit from your tutor
- Summary

Learning objectives

By the end of this chapter you should have a better understanding of:

- The issues surrounding visits from your university tutor
- Being observed by your school-based mentor and colleagues
- Observing others teach
- What constitutes successful observations and visits.

QTS Standards

This chapter is relevant for Standards 7, 8 and 9.

Personal and professional development

Q7 (a) Reflect on and improve their practice, and take responsibility for identifying and meeting their developing professional needs.

Q7 (b) Identify priorities for their early professional development in the context of induction.

Q8 Have a creative and constructively critical approach towards innovation, being prepared to adapt their practice where benefits and improvements are identified.

Q9 Act upon advice and feedback and be open to coaching and mentoring.

Observing others teach

We can learn a great deal from watching others teach. It is something I do a great deal and it never ceases to amaze me the various ways in which teachers communicate with their students and the resources which they develop. I consider it to be a great privilege to do this. When you first go into school, you will usually have the opportunity to observe others teach. For most mentors, it is a way of introducing their trainees to the class and the way things operate within their department and school. You get the chance to observe the norms and, unfortunately, they usually make a very difficult skill look very easy!

Watching a good teacher is like watching a skilled craftsperson or a great actor. They have the class in the palm of their hand and can get them to do whatever they want. Their tasks seem relevant and meaningful, the students seem engaged and keen and a great working atmosphere exists. You may feel a little intimidated by seeing this, wondering how it is you can possibly emulate this success. The one key thing to remember is that your mentor has gone through this exact same process and their skill is the result of a great deal of practice, experience and sheer hard work. They also get it wrong sometimes, so remember that too.

But this is the start of your career, so you need to observe others, find out how the land lies and pick up some handy hints and tips about how to deal with a range of students. The first problem is with the focus, just where do you start? In many cases, your university will give you some school-based tasks which will involve observations and recording those observations. If you are a subject specialist, you will also benefit from seeing other subjects being delivered as well as your own. There are lots of skills being displayed out there, be open to them. It may be useful at this point to read the section on school-based tasks in Chapter 14 on Assignments. This sets out a list of things to look for in an observation and may help you to identify specific aspects to look for.

Obviously, the first thing that you need to do is to arrange an observation with a member of staff. On the whole, teachers are fine with people observing them. Teaching has changed considerably over the past few years from a situation where the classroom was their domain, the door was closed and only opened at the end, with no one but the occupants of the room knowing what had happened in there. Now, being observed is seen as a good thing and part of a continual development process and also the way in which a senior teacher or head of department can ensure high quality teaching. People ask more questions now and rightfully so. Teaching is a huge responsibility and the quality of it should be as high as possible.

Task 9.1

How do you think that the teacher who you are observing thinks about this process?

What are you expecting to get out of the experience of observation?

Effective observation is not an easy task, as there is so much going on in the room. Who are you actually observing? Is it the teacher, or is it the students? What are you observing, the teaching or the learning, and what is the difference? There are so many people in the class, how can you possibly see what they are all doing, and how does the teacher know? You need therefore to have a focus for your observations. You also need a notebook to write down everything that you see. As an observer, you should not be tempted to take an active part in the lesson. You may find this difficult but remember what you are trying to do here, the observation is part of your learning.

It is therefore important to have a plan for your observation and a series of things which you should look for. For your initial observations you may find the following Lesson Observation Sheet useful.

Lesson Observation Sheet

Lesson / Subject

Period   **Year Group**

Number in class

SEN   **G&T**

During the observation, try to find the answers to the following questions:

Was there a starter, if so, what was it?

What were the objectives of the lesson?

What was the focus of the lesson?

What resources were used – help sheets, task sheets, etc?

Was there a plenary, if so, what?

Was there a clear three-part lesson?

These are some of the basic questions which you could use to observe a lesson. However, this only looks at a small part of the lesson, the top level. Once you understand this level, you need to look at the next level of complexity, i.e. what else is happening in the lesson. For a list of additional questions to consider in your observations, turn to Chapter 14 on Assignments and look at the section on school-based tasks.

Task 9.2

Why do you think that it is important to note down the time of the lesson, the age group delivered to and the class make-up in terms of SEN and G&T students?

Using observations of others to guide your teaching

The process of observation and making notes while observing is a powerful learning tool. As indicated earlier, it helps to inform your own learning and allows you to find out some key information about the school and its students. You may wish to discuss your observations with the teacher whose session you observed to find out more. It may be helpful to find out not only what a starter was for but why that particular starter was used.

Observing a number of different teachers allows you to see a range of different techniques used within the classroom. You may see a particular child in a totally different light if he/she is seen in a range of classes. Gaining some ideas is always a good thing. However, try to avoid the temptation to directly copy another teacher's style. It rarely works because you are not being true to you. You may have seen humour used well to help build relationships and motivate students but it may fall flat for you. Look for things like questioning techniques, the effectiveness or otherwise of specific groupings and seating plans, and so forth.

Being observed

Task 9.3

How do you feel about being observed? What are your main concerns? Do you know what your observer is looking for?

Being observed is always a nerve-racking experience as you will automatically feel that you are being judged. This is true of all teachers, even the most experienced ones. No one wants to deliver a poor lesson and we always want to come out of it as a successful and good teacher. This is especially true for the trainee teacher, yet there is so much that is new and so much that you may feel is not under your control. Many trainees who are good at planning and resource development freeze on the spot when first confronted with 'real' students.

One of the first things I wish to stress is that you must be realistic in your expectations. You are new to this and you are a trainee, not a teacher of five years experience with their relationships sorted out. However, being observed is your opportunity to showcase your development so far, receive some coaching on strengths and areas for development as well as a good opportunity to gather evidence for your Standards folder.

You are, of course, being observed all the time by your mentor and your colleagues. However, the formality of a lesson observation obviously puts this into perspective. I hope that through the various chapters of this book, I have stressed the importance of being proactive in the learning process, of taking responsibility for your own personal development as a matter of course. This is also something which you need to do with the programme of observations. Rather than sit back and let your mentor come to you to tell you when you are going to be observed, go to them and ask to be observed with specific groups on specific times. You may also ask for a specific part of the lesson to be observed rather than the whole lesson at the start. So, for example, you may ask your mentor to observe the starter and the plenary activities, or the movement from the starter and introduction to the main activities, a key transition point of a lesson which can make or break it. Build up to the whole lesson by making key parts right and then joining them together.

When you are being observed, make sure that you have copies of all the resources which you will be using in that lesson for both yourself and your mentor. Having a clear and easy to follow lesson plan goes without saying but you also need to make sure that you have the other resources such as seating plans, SEN and G&T details, worksheets which you may use, printouts of PowerPoints and examples of differentiated material which you may have developed. It all helps the person doing the observation to follow the lesson and the train of thought within it. It will also enable the observer to see where problems may arise. In most instances, your mentor may ask for these resources well in advance of the lesson or part lesson so that they can check your levels of preparation and understanding, and that the lesson content is appropriate for the class you will be taking. They may, of course, make suggestions as to how this could be improved and if they do, then act upon this advice, there will be good reason for it.

Be confident, be in control, deliver your lesson to the best of your ability and according to the plan. Once you have done this and the lesson is over, reflect upon it and prepare for the feedback.

Handling feedback

Task 9.4

How do you feel about receiving feedback? What do you want to get out of the feedback?

When an observation has been completed, the next stage in the process should be the feedback. The feedback may not be immediate, your observer may be teaching their own lesson, for example, so be realistic about getting your feedback. Your observer may want to reflect upon what they have seen and do some preparation work for the feedback meeting themselves. However, it is important that you have your feedback as quickly as is feasibly possible and that the feedback should be given to you in an appropriate location, so not in front of a class or with a group of colleagues unless it has been a group observation where you are seeking the opinion of more than one person. I would suggest a private office or meeting room where possible.

In most cases, the first question you will be asked by the observer will be along the lines of 'How did you think the lesson went?'. This is standard practice and gives you the opportunity to make the first comments about the lesson yourself. Your own reflections on the lesson are very important and you will be aware of what went well and what did not work in the way you expected. The more often you go through this process, the fewer surprises there will be. Obviously, at the start of your practice, your mentor may identify a number of areas for you to work on, but hopefully, as your practice progresses, the areas of strength should start to outweigh the targets for improvements. The important thing to remember is that the process is to be used to inform your continual development. You need to be open to the suggestions and to act upon them. This is paramount because it is a key aspect of Standards Q7 and Q9:

Q7 (a)   Reflect on and improve their practice, and take responsibility for identifying and meeting their developing professional needs.

Q9   Act upon advice and feedback and be open to coaching and mentoring.

The reflective process following the observation of your lesson should result in an improved lesson the next time. You should always be evaluating your lessons, identifying the strong points and the areas for development. Feedback from observations is therefore part of this process. Figure 9.1 shows the reflective cycle using observation and feedback.

It is important to stress that the observation process should not be seen as a threatening one, but a supportive and developmental one.

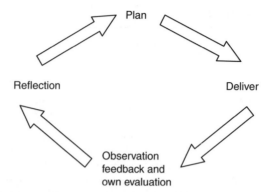

Figure 9.1 Reflective cycle using observation and feedback

Visit from your tutor

As part of your training, you should expect to be visited by your university tutor or a representative of the university. The number of visits depends upon the institution which you are at, however, your mentor may wish to request that your tutor visits more frequently if there is some concern or if the mentor is a little unsure of their judgement and wants guidance on expected Standards. It is important to remember that the university tutor is not simply there for you, it is also a visit to ensure that the mentor is appropriately supported and that the partnership with the university is working well. It is important for trainees to understand that communication between the school and the university is a constant thing. Some students make the mistake of thinking that once they are away from the university, they are on their own and that part of their study is somehow separate. Do not fall into this trap and do not be surprised just how much your tutor knows about your progress in school – it is, after all, another part of their job.

The visit from your tutor should be taken very seriously. This is your chance to show how far you have developed since you have been in the school and how you are applying the theory which you have learned at university. The most important thing is to be fully prepared. Earlier in this chapter, I encouraged you to take control of the observation process by being an active participant in deciding when and with whom you are observed. You should, where possible, adopt the same approach with your university tutor. As you will want to showcase your evolving skills, you could select the date, time and class which you would like them to see. So, after discussing this with your mentor, select appropriate dates and contact your tutor to give her/him the available options.

Your tutor will, of course, want to observe a lesson. This is usually done with the mentor to check that both the tutor and the mentor agree on the overall quality of the lesson. Remember, the tutor will have no prior knowledge of this class, so make sure that they have all the resources that they need at hand. As for your mentor, this should include the lesson plan, the resources you will be using, a seating plan and the levels at which the individual students are performing. Something which the tutor is more likely to do during an observation than your mentor will be to talk to the students about the task they are performing. They may also look at their work in books to see, for example, how you are assessing their work. The observation will last for a full lesson and be very thorough. As with all such observations, there has to be a chance for feedback, so make sure that when you arrange the lesson, there is a suitable time and place for this to occur. Your tutor will also want to have some time with your mentor and possibly the person responsible for trainee teachers in the school to discuss your progress and targets.

Your tutor will also expect to see your teaching files which should contain your lesson plans, resources and your own evaluations as well as any details from previous observations and meetings. They will also be keen to see how you are progressing in terms of collecting the evidence for your QTS Standards, so make sure that you have them with you on that day. It can be very frustrating and show a lack of professionalism if you are not well prepared for this visit. Because of the nature of the visit, I would recommend that you have a checklist and that you make sure that you have all of the boxes ticked before you set off in the morning! I always encourage my trainees to think of it as a mini-Ofsted inspection and treat it accordingly.

Summary

In this chapter we have looked at observations and visits. I hope that you now understand the role of the observation and see it as a positive developmental tool rather than as a threat. I also hope that you can see that, as a professional, you can be very much in control of this whole process, selecting the time and place for observations and even requesting that the observation targets specific parts of the lesson, for example, the starter or the plenary. We have also seen how the observation leads into the reflection and planning process, improving the overall quality of your lesson. We have also looked at the role of the university tutor's visit and you should now have a good understanding of what to expect from this visit and the resources that you should have ready for it.

10 Dealing with failure

Contents

- What does failure mean?
- Failing an assignment
- The critical friend
- Failing your QTS tests
- Failing your placement
- Withdrawing from the course
- Action planning for success
- Appealing
- Summary

Learning objectives

By the end of this chapter I hope you will be able to understand:

- The general principle of failure within the context of your teaching experience
- How to identify a critical friend and what their role should be
- Action planning for success
- How to appeal.

What does failure mean?

Task 10.1

Take time to consider what the word failure means to you. Examine how the word makes you feel and what your concerns, if any, are. If possible, look back at an event which you consider to be a failure and what it was. What have you done to recover from it so that you are where you are now?

Failure is an evocative word. Failure when applied to an individual is even more so. It is a comment that something you have done is not good enough and that you have not met the required Standard, whether that is an assignment, a presentation, or a placement. It is also something which may not be common in your life history. Even the fact that you have gained a place on your teaching course indicates that you are successful. Therefore failure can come as a shock, indicating that something you do is not good enough and that it has not achieved the required Standard. If you do fail a placement, then you are likely to experience a range of emotions: anger, resentment, humiliation, feeling overwhelmed and shocked. Moreover failing a placement can seem worse that failing an assignment for most trainees because it is seen as more personal. And the fact that trainees are graded against professional attributes, skills and knowledge simply emphasizes this.

Mentors are also teachers and teachers do not like failing trainees because they know how much an individual has invested in the course, both personally and financially. Mentors may well put off the difficult situation of telling a trainee that they have not made the grade but, to be honest, this helps no one. We, as teachers, do not like failing people because we know how it makes people feel. Teachers will go out of their way to make people pass if they possibly can, especially if they like the person involved. But passing the course will give you QTS status, which means that you can enter a profession where there is a huge amount of responsibility placed upon you, arguably one of the most important and privileged posts you can occupy. There is no getting away from it; there are minimum standards which must be achieved to ensure that only the best people teach our learners. It is not just about the effort you put in, although a great deal of it is needed. Some people will put in 110 per cent and still not meet the required standards. Having these standards also gives you the opportunity to check if teaching is the profession for you or not. If you are not enjoying the teaching experience and struggling to meet the minimum standards, you need to think long and hard about if this is the right thing for you. If you manage to qualify, it's what you will be doing all day for the foreseeable future. Sometimes, not passing the placement can open doors to a different direction, one more suited to your personality and talents.

Any teaching qualification is intense. You will be scrutinized for your academic ability in terms of the essays which you hand in, as well as your abilities within and beyond the classroom. You will have to become the whole package and this means passing your teaching practice, gathering your QTS status evidence, passing the three QTS tests, as well as your assignments. You are not allowed to become a qualified teacher without these. It does not matter that you have great classroom relationships if your numeracy and literacy are not up to scratch. There is no room for gaps in your evidence or failure to pass your assignments. Your mentors and tutors are there to see that the Standards are met and if you do not meet them, then they will have no option but to say no to you passing the course. If this is the case, then your tutor will have the opportunity to explore what options may be open to you at that point. Some trainees expect to pass the course simply because they have got on to it. This is not the case and you may have to accept that, in the opinion of a number of people, who have given you support, evidenced your progress and worked with you, that teaching simply is not for you. If this is the case, the smart thing to do would be to accept the advice and look for an alternative outlet for your talents. Battling on against the odds may prove fruitless in the long term. I will deal with failing your placement in more depth further in this chapter.

Because of the nature of teaching courses, most of the practice and individual emphasis as far as the trainee is concerned is on the teaching practice. During this time, you will have planned for and delivered a considerable number of lessons, developed resources, marked work and attended parents evenings. In fact, you will have been given many opportunities to provide the evidence for the Standards within the QTS file. However, of equal or greater importance is the academic work which you will have to undergo as part of the course and it is this area which I wish to consider next.

Failing an assignment

Of less emphasis for the trainee appears to be the academic rigour of the university assignments. But without passing these at the required level, you cannot achieve QTS Standard and so become a qualified teacher. There will be a number of assignments and these will differ depending upon the course which you are following. For example, a three-year BEd will be different from the PGCE which in turn differs from students taking the GTP (Graduate Teacher Programme) route. You must make sure that you assign appropriate time and effort to each section of the requirements, whether that is essays, tests or teaching practice to ensure that you pass. Neglect one at your peril and do not leave anything to the last minute. If you do this, it will put you behind with everything on the course and add further pressure to an already pressurized year. However, it is standard practice at universities to allow a student to resubmit work which may have not come up to the required standard. So, if your assignment comes back as 'referred', it is not the end of the world and you do have another chance. If you find yourself in this situation, arrange a tutorial with your university tutor as soon as possible to go through the reasons why you did not meet the standard and what you can do to rectify the situation. Once you have this, act upon it and get the assignment out of the way as quickly as feasibly possible. You may be given a deadline a few months away, but you will be surprised how quickly this time will be eaten into, especially when you have other assignments due in as well as your work for school. I would also strongly recommend that you have a critical friend who will go through the work with you and tell you the truth.

The critical friend

The role of the critical friend is to read through your work and give you an honest opinion of how it reads, how it shapes up to the assessment criteria and where improvements can be made. It is important that they are honest and you are receptive to criticism, otherwise it cannot work and your work may not achieve the Standards it needs. It will also be possible to have your work proof-read at this stage, something which too few people do, with interesting and sometimes humorous results.

Failing your QTS tests

There are three tests: maths, literacy and ICT. They are online tests and, in my opinion, should be done as soon as you can when on the course. They are there to ensure that new teachers meet a minimum standard in these skills. Failing these tests is not uncommon. If you fail one in your specialist topic, it can be embarrassing, but not life-threatening! If you do fail, it is simply a case of rebooking and re-sitting and make sure that you pass next time. If you continue to fail, it may become an issue and you need to see your university tutor to point you towards the support which you may need to get you through the course. But you must pass these tests and pass them before the end of the course to make sure you qualify in time. The exact date for passing does tend to vary and it is up to you to check up on this date.

Failing your placement

The number of placements which you have and the length of those placements will depend upon the particular qualification and university which you are at. For example, Sheffield Hallam University's secondary PGCE courses have two placements, one before Christmas and one running from January to June. Placements are planned to give contrasting experiences so that one may be in a rural, Peak District school followed by an inner city school in Sheffield. The principle is to allow the trainee to experience different types of teaching environments, something which they would not do if they were placed in the same or similar schools for both placements. It also allows the trainee to identify and develop different teaching skills which are needed to enable them to teach across a range of schools.

As already discussed, during your time on placement you will be continually assessed by your mentor and they are required to perform observations, give feedback, and provide training, as well as monitor your progress against your QTS standards and complete your formative and summative reports. The placements are where you demonstrate that you have all of the professional attributes, skills, subject knowledge and understanding to be a teacher and this can only be done by the continual assessment of your practice. This means that, in principle, you should have a good idea of where you are in terms of performance at any time and where you need to focus in terms of your skills as a teacher.

It is unlikely that a trainee will fail their placement practice without the chance to rectify any particular Standard or Standards that they may be struggling with. A likely exception to this may be where a trainee has acted in a manner which would be considered as gross misconduct, for example, striking a child or swearing at a colleague. Examples of what constitutes gross misconduct are covered later on in this chapter. However, both your university and your school should have code of conduct documents which you can refer to and I would advise you to do so prior to placement.

Your mentor may well identify a particular area for development which you may have to work on. For example, your mentor may have observed you on a number of occasions making the same mistake and have given you suggestions of how to deal with this problem. It may seem obvious but take this advice and act upon it, as the advice would come on the back of years of teaching experience and a good understanding of the class in front of you. However, taking advice and acting on it can be difficult for some trainees to take on board. As a result of this, the problem may not be resolved and the trainee is therefore not evidencing professional attribute Standard Q9 which states that you should: 'Act upon advice and feedback and be open to coaching and mentoring'. The solution to this would therefore appear to be an obvious one, take the advice and be seen to follow it. However, it is not simply enough to evidence this Standard once or twice; you must show that you are open to it at all times.

There are many reasons why a trainee can fail a placement, and before I go too far, I only think it is reasonable to consider why this may happen and link it to the QTS Standards.

Reasons for failing your placement

There are many reasons for failing your placement. In some cases, this can be an immediate situation if you have behaved in such an extreme unprofessional manner that you will have your placement terminated immediately. A good example of this would be swearing at a member of staff or striking a child. But these situations are few and far between and, to some extent, obvious. If you are the sort of person who loses control very quickly, the pressures and stresses of teaching are likely to push you to that point at frightening speed, so teaching may not be the profession for you.

On the whole, people tend to fail their placements because they have not met one or more of the QTS Standards. In my experience, it would be reasonable to say that trainees tend to fail on the professional attribute standards Q1–9 or the professional skills standards Q22–33. In professional attributes, it can be any of the 9 Standards; in professional skills, it is usually issues surrounding

Q22 planning, and/or Q30 and Q31 which look at the ability to create a purposeful learning environment and the ability to control the classes that the trainee works with.

In this section, I will look at some of these standards and, drawing on my past experiences and that of other colleagues, indicate the sort of behaviour which leads to failure for specific standards. This way, I would hope that you can see what to avoid!

Meeting the Standards?

Let's start with Standard Q2, one which is often misunderstood by trainees across all routes. This Standard requires you to demonstrate the positive values, attitudes and behaviour they expect from children and young people. The reason given why most people do not understand this is that they are looking at the children rather than themselves, trying to see how the students demonstrate these values. It's not them, it's you!

Task 10.2

What could you do to prove that you are meeting Standard Q2, demonstrating the positive values, attitudes and behaviour they expect from children and young people?

What would a trainee do if they were failing to meet this standard?

This Standard is about how you present yourself, how you, as a responsible adult, model what you want from your students. Is it reasonable to expect your students to come to the lesson on time, well prepared in a calm manner, if you do not do so yourself? Of course not. This is arguably one of the easiest Standards to demonstrate. It is simply about being there, being there on time, being organized and behaving in a manner which you expect your students to emulate, even if they don't always do it themselves. If you don't expect the students to shout at each other, then try to avoid it yourself. If you expect students to dress appropriately, then make sure you do.

Demonstrating that you are aware of the professional duties of teachers (Q3) means that you should be, at the very least, making sure you take the register, keep your records up to date, that you are there on time, that you attend appropriate meetings and so forth.

Communicating with children, young people, colleagues, parents and carers (Q4) is another Standard which presents problems for some trainees. They may be comfortable with one group but not others or may be fine at communication in the classroom and staffroom, but not contacting parents, especially if the information to be given is not good news. It is important to note that this Standard talks about communication with a wide group of people and this is a key skill for a teacher to possess.

Task 10.3

How would you evidence that you can communicate effectively with:

• children?

• young people?

• colleagues?

• parents and carers?

The ability to communicate with this group is vital. Trainees often struggle with communicating with children and young people at first. It can be tricky, they are not in your normal peer group and so you have to learn to adjust. In some instances, you have come directly from a university course or in some circumstances, direct from industry. Consequently, you will not have been exposed to groups of young children. A common mistake therefore is to pitch not only the language you use but the tasks you set at too high a level. For most trainees, this lesson is one learnt very quickly and they learn to adjust. The problem in this instance would be you either do not recognize that there is an issue, or if you fail to rectify it. The difficulty in communication will normally be picked up very quickly by your mentor and other staff and addressed via observations and when you are aware of it, it is usually a simple problem to rectify. The first advice would be to try to model the way your mentor speaks to the students.

Communicating with colleagues can also be an issue. A common complaint from mentors is that the trainee simply did not pass on information about days at university, for example, or pass on messages from other members of staff or parents or withheld key information. Generally with issues of staff conduct, there will be a document stating your responsibilities regarding communication. So, for example, if you are going to be ill or unavoidably detained, you will be expected to notify the school immediately you are aware of the situation. Make sure you are aware of the contact details and use them accordingly. This sort of mistake is usually made by the new trainee and is unintentional. This said, if you do fail to follow procedure, apologize and assure your mentor that it will not happen again. It is important to remember that a school runs smoothly on shared information, especially when that information helps colleagues and prevents them making mistakes. If, for example, information about a child being late for school for a medical appointment is not passed on by you to the host teacher or school office, the parent may receive an embarrassing phone call asking why their child is not at school. Another communication issue which arises is that of the over-confident trainee who has an opinion on everything and is happy to share it with the whole staffroom. Needless to say, a trainee who tells everyone that according to their experience, what someone is saying is wrong, is inevitably going to cause conflict and impact badly on the harmony of the workplace.

The third communication issue is that of communicating with parents and carers. Obviously, if there is a serious issue to deal with, it will be handled by a more experienced member of staff. However, there are times when you will have to communicate with parents and carers and you have to think carefully how you do this. As one of the Standards, you have to evidence it and I would suggest that you have to evidence that you can do it in a number of ways. The first and most obvious of these is the parents evening. This is where you can prove to your mentor that you can communicate important information in a professional manner. Therefore, you should take this opportunity when it presents itself to you. You will usually be with the host teacher for the parents evening and the host teacher will be expected to take the lead. However, you may well find that you will be expected to give comments or take the lead yourself at times. Do not appear disinterested, grumble about attending or make inappropriate comments! Also remember that 90 per cent of communication is in your body language. Your presentation is therefore as vital here as in the classroom and you should dress appropriately.

You may also be expected to contact a student's home, something which is always easier to do if the information to present is good rather than bad. All parents want to hear good things about their children and most will assume the worst when the school phones home. Therefore, it is important to be prepared, know what you want to say and have any important information at your fingertips.

The first thing to do is to make sure that you are speaking to the right person. There are many occasions when teachers have not checked and then have proceeded to speak to an older brother or sister. Once you have confirmed that you have the right person, you should then check that it is alright to speak at this time, it may be inconvenient at that time, in which case, ask when it would be more convenient and call back later. If you have the right person and the right time, you should then discuss in a friendly but professional way the issue at hand. Obviously, if it is a difficult or sensitive area, it may be more appropriate for a senior member of staff to handle it. However, you may be contacting as a sanction following some behaviour issues within the class. Parents will naturally be defensive about their child and want all of the available facts about the incident before they respond. Remember, you are passing information on and you may be requesting permission for a further sanction such as a detention. You are not in a position to request that the parent issues a further sanction; it is up to them to take such action if they think appropriate. One thing that you must always do is remain calm and make sure that the phone call ends as professionally as it started.

It would be wrong to complete this section without saying something about confidentiality. Obviously, as a trainee, you will have access to a great deal of information about staff and students alike. Discussing these issues at inappropriate times, with the wrong people, or in the wrong location may well be considered to be breaking confidentiality, something which is covered later in the section on gross misconduct.

For Standard Q7 (a), you are expected to take responsibility for your own professional development, to reflect upon and improve your practice. As your placements progress, you will be expected to do more and more of this. At the start of your practice, you may not be aware of how to improve your practice and what you should be doing. This is despite the fact that this is the point when you know the least and have most to learn.

Task 10.4

Looking at Q7 (a), what could you do to demonstrate to your mentor that you are meeting or working towards achieving this Standard?

A failing or weak trainee in this instance is one who is just sitting back and taking no personal responsibility for their development. All trainees have areas for development, whether that is subject knowledge, behaviour management, assessment techniques or resource development for all students, so you should be seen to be doing something about it. Areas for development will be identified by those who work with you, but you will also be aware of them yourself. For example, perhaps you have been working with a new class and you have a student who is experiencing some difficulty in accessing the lesson. A weak trainee would do nothing. The stronger trainee would demonstrate that they are meeting this standard by first talking to their mentor about the situation and then going to the internet or university library to find out how they could help this student and then implement their findings. Evidencing this standard is fairly straightforward and should quickly become standard practice.

Of all of the professional Standards attributes, the one which most trainees fail on is Q9, acting upon advice and mentoring and be open to coaching and mentoring. A trainee who is failing to meet this standard is simply not open to taking and acting on advice. Also frequently this is found to be the trainee who has an opinion on all things and will not listen to others.

Task 10.5

How could you demonstrate to your mentor that you are meeting the requirements of Standard Q9?

As a trainee, you have to be open to mentoring and coaching and you have to take advice and act on it. You are working with a mentor who not only has good experience of teaching but who also knows the school and its students too. It is in your interest to act on this. So basically, if your mentor does give you some advice or guidance, act on it and do what they suggest.

So far in this section, I have been looking at some of the Standards from the professional attributes section and possible reasons why trainees fail. I have also made some simple suggestions about how you could evidence that you are working on these Standards. My experience would seem to suggest that fewer trainees fail their placements by not meeting Standards in the professional knowledge and understanding section. However, this is not to say that it does not happen and if it is the case, then it tends to be linked to other Standards, usually Q9, when a trainee has been given advice about how to resolve a different Standard and not acted upon it. On the whole, trainees who are teaching a specific subject, science or ICT, for example, tend to have the subject knowledge for the subjects they teach, or, if they do not, they can find out. In primary, where a trainee is supposed to be able to teach across a range of subjects, trainees again will make sure they are sufficiently skilled to teach the subjects which they are expected to deliver. If you are not, and do nothing about it, then you are not taking the responsibility for developing your needs as identified in Standard Q7.

The most common areas for failure in the professional knowledge and understanding section are Q12 ('Know a range of approaches to assessment including the importance of formative assessment'), Q18 ('Understand how children and young people develop') and Q19 ('Know how to make effective personalized provision for those they teach'). The Standards demonstrated in this section tend to be developed as the placements continue and it may not be possible to demonstrate your proficiency in them in the same way that you can do with professional attributes, many of which can be displayed from day one. For example, Standard Q12 requires the trainee not only to demonstrate their understanding of assessment and the different methods, but also the importance of formative assessment and the consequences of being skilled in this area.

Task 10.6

Standard Q12 requires a trainee to demonstrate their understanding of different assessment methods and the importance of formative assessment. How would a strong trainee demonstrate this to their mentor?

A weak trainee may avoid assessment in traditional ways such as the physical marking of books and other work. The trainee may also simply give a mark and not identify how to improve the work the next time. They may find it difficult to conduct the formative assessment of the classroom via effective questioning, working directly with a child to help them not to understand where they are at the moment, but also how to move themselves to the next level. These are skills which have to be developed and demonstrated over a longer period of time. An effective teacher does this as second nature whereas a trainee may take time to develop this. Mentors therefore are looking for a trainee who is developing these skills, moving forward with them, seeking help and advice at developing such skills.

As indicated earlier, my experience has highlighted Standards Q18 and Q19 as areas where trainees may fall down. Basically, a trainee failing Standards Q18 and Q19 will be one who displays no insight into the environment in which their students are growing up in and what influence that has on their development. The student will learn outside school as well as inside school and the values and beliefs of their local culture will impact on how children learn. A student who comes from a background of social and economic depravation will not have the same opportunities and life experiences as a child from a more financially comfortable environment. The trainee needs to be aware of this and sensitive to it. A good trainee will understand the importance of the Every Child Matters agenda (Every Child Matters, Green Paper, 2003) and the importance of personalization in a child's educational development.

As above, the Professional Knowledge and Understanding Standards tend not to be ones where most trainees fall down. This is because this is more directly within the trainee's control than some aspects of the Professional Attributes, which may require a change of personality, mindset and habits which have formed over a lifetime and consequently are more difficult to change. However, the Professional Skills area is somewhere that a number of trainees may also fail to meet the Standards. As with the Professional Knowledge and Understanding section, mentors will not expect you to be master of these at the start of your placement, but will expect these to develop and continue to develop as the placement continues and as a consequence of experience, advice and your own research into aspects of your own professional development. For example, it is important that any teacher has a good working relationship with his/her students, that classroom discipline is established and that a safe and positive working environment is the norm within the classroom. If you do not have this, it will make it very difficult to teach.

Task 10.7

If you were observing a lesson, how would you know if the lesson was in control, if the behaviour of the students was acceptable and that a positive working environment has been established?

In terms of Standards, these behavioural issues relate directly to Q30 and Q31 and they are a must for every teacher. At the start, trainees will find this difficult, not only because the responsibility for controlling 30 individuals is a new thing, but also that students see trainees as 'fair game' and will try to push the boundaries to see how far they can go before they settle down. Think back to the time when you were a student. How did you treat the trainee teachers? However, this testing period settles down and it's what happens after that which is important, how quickly can you impose yourself on your class to make a positive working environment? Some trainees never manage to master this skill and consequently they may fail on these Standards alone. To avoid this, find out what strategies work for the individuals in the class. Make sure that your lessons are well planned and stimulating. Make sure you know the school's behaviour policy and use it. Think about your seating plans and groupings. Be confident, positive and take control.

Another area where trainees tend to fail is in their planning (Q22). A failing student will not be very skilled in this area, or may try to avoid planning at all. It is not unusual for trainees to return to university sessions complaining that they do not see their mentor's lesson plans, or that if they have them, they may be prompts in the form of a bullet point list. This being the case, a weak trainee may argue against producing plans, seeing this as unfair. However, this obviously shows a lack of insight on behalf of the trainee. Your mentor will have had a number of years of teaching experience and will know exactly what they are going to teach within that lesson. The fact that it may not be committed to paper may mean that it is committed to their memory. They would no doubt be able to produce a high quality lesson plan if so required and will do when they have to introduce a new topic or one which they are not too comfortable with. Again, this is something that has to be developed. You will no doubt have covered lesson planning at university. However, there is often a gap between theory and practice. Some universities insist on their students using the university lesson plan style, others leave it up to the school to decide the structure and nature of content. Whatever the situation, you will have to adjust quickly to the requirements of the school. If you are doing a PGCE, and you are on your second placement, the school may give you a little time to adjust to their structure, but they will expect you to know the basics of planning the content of the lesson and the development of appropriate resources. Many mentors will also expect you to submit your lesson plans to them before you teach the lesson, usually a minimum of 48 hours. This is to allow the mentor to check what you are doing and guide you to make adjustments if needed. If you are advised to make changes, please do this as it is strong evidence for Standard Q9, arguably the Standard which is at the heart of many failures.

In the first instance, you will use a lesson-by-lesson approach, but you will quickly be expected to see the lesson as one of a group and be able to create a longer-term plan in which your individual lesson will sit. Effective planning is a key skill. Do it well, and it will impact on your teaching as a whole. The 2009 Steer Report on issues of Behaviour Management went so far as to suggest that if you get the planning right, behaviour will not be a problem in the class. While I have issues with this in terms of a consideration of what affects pupil behaviour, there can be no doubt that if a teacher is thoroughly prepared, with a plan which takes into account the needs and learning styles of the individuals within the group, the battle is nearly won.

It is fair to say that you can, as a trainee, fail your placement by not evidencing one or more of the Standards, depending on having a realistic opportunity to display them. The further you are into your placements, the more competent you will be expected to be at demonstrating your skills. However, the most frequent reasons for students failing their placements is their lack of professional behaviour, their unwillingness to act on advice, their lack of awareness and empathy with their students, their failure to communicate with staff, their inability to create relationships with students, poor planning and poor classroom control.

The 'cause for concern' document

If you were a student at Sheffield Hallam University (SHU) and you consistently fail to act upon advice or are failing to meet one or more of the Standards, then your mentor may issue a 'cause for concern' (different institutions will have different versions of the same document) which will tell you exactly where you are going wrong, what you are expected to do about it, and outline the support which may be given to help you. This will also have a date given to it by which time you will be expected to consistently meet the target. The university will have been informed of this and your mentor will be well aware of the situation. Figure 10.1, an example of a 'Cause for Concern' form, clearly indicates the Standards which need to be addressed, the proposed action to be taken by the trainee and the review date.

At the end of the period stated for the cause for concern, you will have a meeting with your mentor, and usually your university tutor to discuss progress and next stages. If you have failed to act upon the advice and continued to be unable to demonstrate that you are now meeting the Standards specified, a number of things may happen. If you have clearly started to show some improvement, your mentor may decide to extend your deadline to see if you can meet them, given additional time. Your mentor may give you more targets to meet with a new deadline. Alternatively, if you are failing to make sufficient progress despite the best efforts of your mentor and yourself, you may have your placement terminated by the partner school. This may mean that you have, in effect, failed the placement part of the course and the option of being given another placement at another school may not be available to you. If this is the case, then your mentor may well advise you to leave the course.

However, let us assume that you, like many students who receive a C4C, have managed to resolve the issue(s) that your mentor identified and that you have completed your teaching practice. At the end of the practice, your mentor will sit down with you and complete your summative review (see Chapter 8 for details) during which they will identify strengths and areas for development. This document will then be sent to the university and be subject to scrutiny via one of the progression boards which sit to ratify if a student can progress to their next placement, or in the event of the final board, if they have met the Standards required to pass the course and become a qualified teacher.

CAUSE FOR CONCERN (C4C)

Trainee: ...   **Course: PGCE ICT**

School/College: ...   **Term: 1 2 3 [*please circle*]**

Mentor: **Date:**

	Section of the Standards	Summary of weakness (Please identify Q.. and give brief) details)	Summary of proposed action and dates
S1	Professional Attitudes Q1–Q9 • Relationships with Children • Frameworks • Communication and Working with Others • Personal and Professional Development	Q9 Act on advice and be open to coaching and mentoring – not reacting sufficiently to advice. Q7 a and b Reflect upon and improve their practice, take responsibility for identifying professional needs, identify priorities for development. Not identifying and acting upon personal development, especially those concerning behaviour management and resource development as identified in lesson observations.	To act upon advice given and implement instructions. Specifically to do with planning and school procedures to do with lesson delivery. Research appropriate literature and websites for advice and resources. Arrange for and conduct observation of specified members of staff to identify good practice. **Proposed Review Date:**

Figure 10.1 A Cause for Concern form *(continued)*

S2	Professional Knowledge and Understanding Q10–Q21 • Teaching and Learning • Assessment and Monitoring • Subjects and Curriculum • Literacy, Numeracy & ICT • Achievement and Diversity • Health and Well-being	Q12 Know a range of opportunities for assessment, including the importance of formative assessment. At the moment, you are missing opportunities for assessment within the classroom environment and not showing an understanding how its effective use can act as a motivational tool and a method of building positive relationships and a good working environment.	Develop your understanding and use of formative assessment techniques, especially peer assessment and the use of students' work as exemplar materials. Make sure that assessment is included in your planning. **Proposed Review Date:**
S3	Professional Skills Q22–Q33 • Planning • Teaching • Assessing, Monitoring and Giving Feedback • Reviewing Teaching and Learning • Learning Environment • Team Working and Collaboration	Q22–planning Planning needs development at the moment and shows some gaps. You need to make sure that plans are sufficiently developed for the lessons you teach. Think about what learning is going on, what are you doing to promote that learning, identify opportunities for assessment, differentiate resources and think about the timing of the lesson.	Make sure your plans are developed and given to your mentor 48 hours in advance of the lesson to be delivered. Make sure that all elements of the plan are complete and ensure that **ALL details** are available to observers – class lists, details of current levels, seating plan, all resources to be used, as well as the plan.

Figure 10.1 (continued)

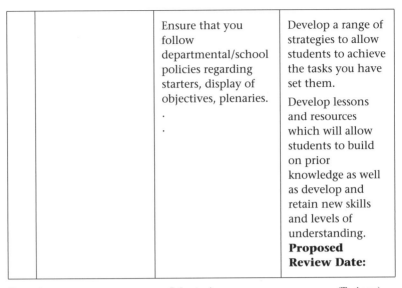

		Ensure that you follow departmental/school policies regarding starters, display of objectives, plenaries. · ·	Develop a range of strategies to allow students to achieve the tasks you have set them. Develop lessons and resources which will allow students to build on prior knowledge as well as develop and retain new skills and levels of understanding. **Proposed Review Date:**

Signed: .... (Mentor) .... (Trainee)
Keep your original and give a photocopy to the trainee and a photocopy to the moderator or send a photocopy to the Partnership Team.

Figure 10.1 *(continued)*

Depending upon what has been written on the summative report, especially if they have a C4C, trainees will either progress to the next placement without condition, progress to the next placement with clear targets, be recommended that they make no further progress (in effect fail), or qualify as a teacher. As we are looking at issues of dealing with failure, I intend to follow the path of a trainee who has been allowed to continue into a practice, but with conditions attached.

Gross misconduct

I have mentioned the issue of gross misconduct earlier. Anyone whose conduct comes under this umbrella is in a situation where they can be suspended or dismissed if they are employed, or removed immediately from placement in the case of a trainee teacher. Your university and school will both have clear documentation which outlines what is considered as gross misconduct, and you should be aware of these before you go on placement. However, it would only be reasonable to outline some of the issues which fall into this category. Most of them would appear to be obvious. However, there are some situations where a trainee may feel that they are hard done by as they are still a student themselves. However, this is a professional course and you have responsibilities which may mean that what is acceptable for some students is not for the trainee teacher.

Task 10.8

What does gross misconduct mean to you? If you were asked to describe an incidence of gross misconduct, what examples could you think of?

The examples given below are not all inclusive, they are a sample. However, it is important to note that such conduct is considered a breach of contractual terms. Some would result in instant dismissal if you were a qualified teacher.

- Offences of dishonesty, including theft and fraud.
- Racial offences committed at work and/or outside working hours.
- Fighting/physical violence.
- Deliberate falsification of records such as expenses claims, qualifications, etc.
- Deliberate damage to property.
- Serious incapability while on duty, brought on by alcohol or illegal drugs.
- Serious insubordination.
- Serious breach of confidence (subject to the Public Interest (Disclosure) Act, 1998).
- Insubordination, i.e. when an employee is insubordinate by word or gesture/action.
- Abuse of authority, i.e. when an employee's conduct towards a fellow employee or member of the public is oppressive or abusive.
- Absence from duty without good reason (including lateness) and absence from duty without permission or good reason to leave his/her place of work.
- Smoking on Council premises where smoking is prohibited.
- Cumulative Misconduct. A series of misconduct issues.

As you can see from these examples, there are lots of things to consider. However, I do feel that most of these should be obvious to any trainee.

Withdrawing from the course

You may, of course, choose to withdraw from the course. You can do this as a temporary or permanent action. A permanent withdrawal is exactly what it says, you are leaving the course. You may have come to this decision based on your experiences and expectations, or you may be coached on this action by your mentor and university tutor. You may simply have come to the decision that teaching is not for you. That's fine. As a profession, teaching can be rewarding in the extreme. If your heart is not in it, it can be one of the most miserable experiences. Better to remove yourself now and re-evaluate your life's direction.

A temporary withdrawal is something quite different. This says that you want to continue with the course, but at this moment in time, you are not able to give it your best so you need time to regroup and come back to the course when you are in a stronger position. Reasons for a temporary withdrawal may be that you have experienced a period of ill health and so are finding it difficult to keep up with the work. You may have to support a family member more than you thought you would have to. You may be in a position where you are aware that you are not up to completing the course and may need some more experiences in the classroom as a classroom assistant rather than the responsibilities of a teacher to make you a stronger candidate. As a temporary withdrawal is something to be discussed and agreed with your university tutor, it is not something which can be used to simply avoid failing the course and may only be granted if there is good reason and your tutor can see that this is a positive and practical step to take.

Action planning for success

Being under the spotlight because you are not up to the required standard is not a good position to be in. It is uncomfortable, you may feel resentful, it may be the first time you have ever been in this situation. However, you must be reflective about this. Your mentors and tutors have not specified specific requirements unreasonably. You have not evidenced the Standards in sufficient depth to allow you to become a teacher unless you address them. The first thing to ask yourself should be 'Do I want to do anything about this? Do I really want to become a teacher?'

If the answer to both questions is yes, then read on, if no, close the book, put it down and start to plan your life down a different route, no one will think any the less of you for making that decision. The worst thing to do is do nothing. If you think that the issue raised is not a problem and you will not change, then you will fail and it is no one's fault but your own. I feel that if you do have specific targets, it puts you in a position of personal power because it is up to you to plan your way out, to do something positive and become a better person because of it.

If you have a target set, then your placement will be aware of it and you should discuss this in an open and honest manner with your mentor as soon as possible to identify why you have a target set and specify how you will resolve this problem. I would always recommend that you look at the TDA website at the Standards and how you can evidence them before you have this meeting. The website for this is: http://www.tda.gov.uk/partners/ittstandards/guidance_08/qts.aspx.

Either way, as long as the system of requiring evidence continues, there will be a site to support it. You should do this for a number of reasons. First, it will give you ideas, second, it will show your mentor that you are serious about resolving the issue, and, third, it puts you in control. If you take this approach, then you are more likely to achieve your objective and continue to progress to achieving QTS status. If you do not, then you have made another clear decision and one which is in your own long-term interests.

If you have had targets set to your progression, then there will be a deadline to review if the targets have either been met or are being worked towards and that your new mentor is happy for you to proceed.

Appealing

You may have gone through the whole process, written your assignments, completed your QTS tests and tried to gather your QTS Standards. However, you may still have failed to pass the course and have been advised that you cannot make further progress. For some, this may be a blessed relief that they do not have to pursue a career which they were not suited to. However, some feel that they have to challenge this for some reason. This may be a dubious one driven by personal pride, or it may be for a more reasonable reason such as feeling that the reason that they failed was that the mentor did not give them the opportunity to prove that they were up to Standard or that the bar had been set too high for them.

In either situation, you will have to ask yourself the questions 'What am I appealing about? What evidence do I have of supporting my appeal?' If you are clear, and you have the evidence to back up your appeal, then you will have to follow procedure and submit your appeal to the university through the appropriate channels, which differ from university to university. Your university student union will be able to help you as will student administration for your department. It usually takes some time for the appeals to be heard, and you may not receive the reply you hoped for. However, if your appeal is successful, then you will get another opportunity to meet the requirements for teacher status.

Summary

In this chapter we have looked at the issues surrounding failure, be it an assignment, QTS test or your teaching practice, and also identified action which you can take to improve your situation or turn it around completely. Again, as with other chapters in this book, we have seen the role that you, as an active participant in the process, can take through action planning to appeals.

Part II

Professional Skills

So far, the content of this book has concentrated more on the emotional side of your experiences on your teaching practice. However, it is not possible to look at this side alone. To survive your teaching practice, there will be a number of practical issues which you will experience, each of which will impact on your ability to teach effectively. If I did not touch on these issues, I would be neglecting some of the key aspects which impact on your practice. In this section, I will look at issues of planning, assessment, teaching and learning using ICT, and your own assignments. As with the previous chapters, I will link the content to the QTS Standards and hope that, through the content of the chapters and the tasks in them, you will have a better understanding of how to approach these key parts of your practice.

11 Lesson planning

Contents

- Introduction to lesson planning
- What makes a good plan?
- The link between the plan and the scheme of work
- Teaching and learning
- Pre-planning
- Planning your lesson – what should you include?
- All, most, some
- Linking the lesson to the structure
- Using breakout points
- Evaluation
- Summary
- Further reading
- Useful websites

Learning objectives

By the end of this chapter you should:

- Understand the importance of a good lesson plan on classroom management
- Understand the basic structure of a lesson plan
- Understand the concept of the breakout point in planning
- Understand the importance of your class within your plan
- Understand Personalized Learning
- Understand the difference between learning and teaching styles and how to accommodate them in your lesson.

QTS Standards

The chapter is particularly relevant to Q Standards 7(a), 8, 10, 15, 19, 22 and 25(c).

Personal and professional development

Q7 (a) Reflect on and improve their practice, and take responsibility for identifying and meeting their developing professional needs.

Q8 Have a creative and constructively critical approach towards innovation, being prepared to adapt their practice where benefits and improvements are identified.

Teaching and learning

Q10 Have a knowledge and understanding of a range of teaching, learning and behaviour management strategies and know how to use and adapt them, including how to personalise learning and provide opportunities for all learners to achieve their potential.

Subjects and curriculum

Q15 Know and understand the relevant statutory and non-statutory curricula, frameworks, including those provided through the National Strategies, for their subjects/curriculum areas, and other relevant initiatives applicable to the age and ability range for which they are trained.

Achievement and diversity

Q19 Know how to make effective personalised provision for those they teach, including those for whom English is an additional language or who have special educational needs or disabilities, and how to take practical account of diversity and promote equality and inclusion in their teaching.

Planning

Q22 Plan for progression across the age and ability range for which they are trained, designing effective learning sequences within lessons and across series of lessons and demonstrating secure subject/curriculum knowledge.

Teaching

Q25 Teach lessons and sequences of lessons across the age and ability range for which they are trained in which they:

   (c) adapt their language to suit the learners they teach, introducing new ideas and concepts clearly, and using explanations, questions, discussions and plenaries effectively.

Introduction to lesson planning

In this chapter I will be looking at issues surrounding the planning of lessons. At the start of this book, I intended to steer away from issues such as effective planning because I felt that I should be concentrating on issues such as relationships with student and staff, behaviour management and your own time management. However, it is evident that the effective planning of lessons and resource content have a direct impact on this and consequently some of the issues at least should be covered.

Effective planning is at the centre of effective teaching. As the Steer Report implies, get the planning right and the behaviour will not be a problem. If you don't plan, how can you teach? How do you know the structure of the lesson, what should happen when? How do you know what resources to use? Planning and the evaluation of that plan are key requirements of your teaching practice. You are expected to produce a plan for every lesson which you do. At first, these plans may not be the best, but they will develop with practice and experience and an understanding of what it is that you have to do within a lesson.

What makes a good plan?

One of the most common things that trainees comment on is that when they are out in schools, they do not see evidence of full and expansive lesson plans for each lesson. They make the mistake of thinking that the teacher they are observing does not plan and therefore think that planning is not as important as stated at university. The reality of the situation is that the trainee has been watching a skilled teacher deliver without an explicit plan in front of them. They may not have the piece of paper with them every time, but they have certainly planned the lesson they are delivering and are very aware of what is going on, when, how and why. They will be clear on issues of SEN within the class and will have developed appropriate differentiated resources. When these teachers are asked to produce plans, they produce very high quality ones indeed. The difference is when you see a weak teacher attempt this technique of teaching without a paper plan but they usually fall flat on their face.

A good plan is therefore the product of a great deal of thought and preparation and, if the lesson is delivered a number of times, it will be refined and honed as a result of personal evaluation and a process of trial and error. The most important thing about a lesson plan is that it can be and is used, that it's not a piece of paper with words on which has no impact on your teaching or your students' learning. Lesson plans themselves will vary from institution to institution and school to school. While on placement, the plan you use will be the one agreed between the university and the partnership school. Some schools insist that the trainee follow the school's standard plan, some universities insist that their own plans are used. Consequently, you can expect to see a range of plans during your teaching. However, the basic points are the same within every plan.

Each plan should state the objectives and proposed outcomes of the lesson, the activities which will go on through the lesson, and what resources are needed. It should also give details of the make-up of the class, the year group, the gender splits, the make-up of the group in terms of their ability. But these are the basics. Most lesson plans are much more detailed than this and you can expect to spend at least double the amount of time which you will teach a lesson to the planning of it. As you become more skilled at this activity, it will reduce in time but at the start, it is a very difficult task. To do it effectively, you need to strip back to the basics.

The link between the plan and the scheme of work

Whatever you are teaching, you will be working within a scheme of work which will look at a subject at a high level over a number of teaching sessions which link together. Delivering a one-off lesson is not a common situation. Therefore when you are planning a lesson, you will link back to previous lessons learning and form a bridge to further learning via the lesson you will deliver in that session.

Task 11.1

What do you think are the differences between teaching and learning? What teaching activities do you think should be contained within a lesson? How do you think that students will demonstrate that they have learnt within a lesson?

Teaching and learning

Before you start the whole process of planning, you have to strip back to basics to gain a good understanding of the process. I feel that one of the key points which you must be clear about is the difference between teaching and learning, and who is doing what and when.

Task 11.2

Think back to when you were a student in the classroom. What different teaching styles did you observe?

How effective were they in terms of stimulating your learning?

By doing this short exercise, you will no doubt be able to identify a number of different teaching styles which you will have experienced. You may have come up against the facilitator style teacher who sets you a task and enables you to take this forward via discussing your solutions and supporting you in developing your answers to the question posed. You may have experienced the demonstrator who explains and demonstrates a solution, and then expects you to emulate it in some way. This is very common in more practical, skill-based topics such as PE technology or ICT. You may have come across a more dictatorial style where a teacher simply talks at you or gives you work to do from a book and you are expected to take notes or work to a very tight deadline where there is little interaction.

I think that it is reasonable to say that, although these teaching styles exist, modern-day teachers, although they may have a preference for a specific teaching approach, have to be flexible and adjust their teaching to the task at hand and the class they are teaching. You, as a trainee teacher, will certainly have to be flexible in your approach as effectiveness in teaching is increasingly judged by what the students have learnt, rather than how the teacher teaches, although there is of course a link. This means that you as the teacher have to adapt to the learning styles of the students themselves, not as a group, but as individuals within that group. One size does not fit all. If you try one approach and it does not work for some of your students, you must have a different approach for them.

We all have different preferences for our learning styles. The fact that you are on a teacher training course clearly indicates that you have successfully negotiated the education system thus far with its emphasis on proving understanding via written examinations. You are likely to be a multi-skilled learner, able to adapt to the situation you are in. You have also matured and will be able to motivate yourself to work rather than be directed to the task as you would have been as a young person.

The learning styles of children are, however, different from those of adults. If you are teaching to GCSE and beyond, you will also be teaching in that transition period between child and adult where they may demonstrate some of the more mature learning skills, but retain some of the more child-centred ones. Psychologists such as Jerome Bruner (1966) would stress the importance of the teacher's role in facilitating the mental growth of the student. It should therefore be clear that the lessons you deliver and therefore the plans you develop will reflect these levels of development, that the more mature and able student should be able to learn more and perform more cerebrally complex tasks the older they get.

On the whole, teachers tend to talk about three separate learning styles: kinaesthetic, visual and auditory learners. What this means is that students who are kinaesthetic tend to prefer a hands-on approach and are more likely to learn best in this fashion. They may lose concentration if there is little external simulation and consequently may not perform well in class if they are required to simply work from a book. Unfortunately, some teachers will see this as a problem for the child and may see them as being disruptive rather than see that the problem is the way that they have planned their lesson has not taken into account the learning style of this individual.

An auditory learner works best when they are talking a situation through and are given lots of prompts from the teacher. Such students often like to have the situation clearly explained to them, have the opportunity to perform an activity, and then have a change to feedback and debrief on it. Such learners will benefit from opportunities to work in groups, undertake activities such as brainstorming and question and answer sessions. They may not, however, be as strong with reading and writing tasks.

Visual learners tend to learn best via the written word and as a result, perform well in situations where they are expected to undertake written or reading tasks. As a result of this, they tend to be seen as the more compliant student because they are more likely to get on with the written tasks which others may see as dull. It is also important to remember that the education system tends to lean towards these types of learners as we tend to formally assess via the written word rather than other styles.

This is not to say that your students will have one learning style and one alone, they will not. They will have a preference. However, it is important to recognize the differences and, via your planning and delivery, allow all students to demonstrate their ability to learn by preparing appropriate activities for them. It is also important to remember the recent emphasis on the personalized learning of each student. Personalized learning requires considerable knowledge on the part of the teacher about the students in their class. This should enable them to identify a student's strengths and areas for development and to use this information to inform planning and therefore raise the student's confidence and competence. The move is therefore away from the class as a whole towards the needs of the individual within that class.

Pre-planning

Task 11.3

What information would you like to have before you start to plan your lesson?

I think that it is important to think of the information you would like to have available to you before you start teaching. For the trainee teacher, I would argue that one of the most important pieces of knowledge you would want would be a grasp of the class you will be teaching. As a trainee, you will normally have the luxury of meeting your classes before you take them over. This is normally done by shadowing the teacher in the lesson for a short period and acting as a teaching assistant. This will obviously give you the opportunity to find out about the individuals within the group. Make sure that you talk to the host teacher about the group, find out their names, and assessment details you may have and as much about the students as you can. You should be careful about taking on board the personal opinions of individuals within the class from the host teacher, but being forewarned is generally a good thing. You may find that you like the individual that you have been told is a nightmare pupil who does no work.

Once you have a good understanding of the class, be clear about at what stage you will be taking the class over. It is always a good thing to start at a new topic if possible so that you can take it from there. It is always more difficult to take over part-way through, although this may be unavoidable, especially if your students are working to a tight deadline such as project work for assessment in Y10. The third thing you need to understand is the scheme of work which your students are working towards. Are they looking at the Vikings in Y5 history, Photosynthesis in Y8 science or Keats in Y12 English? Once you have these three things, you will be ready to start to plan your lessons.

Planning your lesson – what should you include?

As indicated earlier in this chapter, different schools will have different formats for their lesson plans and as a result, they may expect you to include different information. However, it is important to include key details into your plan. As you can see from Figure 11.1, there are a number of basic details about the class as well as details of the activities and objectives of that class.

At the top of the plan will be the details of the class itself, the year group, the date and time of the lesson, the make-up of the class in terms of gender split, identification of any SEN and G&T students who may be in the group. All of this data is fairly standard, but it is important that it be included. A good lesson plan should allow any competent teacher to take your lesson for you, so detail is good.

However, it is the detail of this lesson which you then need to go on to. Obviously, you need to establish what it is that you are going to teach and where you want your students to be at the end of the lesson. A common problem experienced by most trainees is getting the pitch and pace of the lesson right and a frequent problem is that of overcomplicating things. The lesson may assume a level of understanding at university level rather than that of an 11-year-old. Another common problem is the amount that the trainee is expecting their students to learn. Fearful of running out of material, they try to pack five hours work into one. If this happens to you, don't panic! Most teachers have made this same mistake themselves and it is one that experience helps resolve very quickly. Identifying what you want by the end

LESSONPLANNINGSHEET

Date		Period	3	Teacher	AB	Asst(s)	0	Year/Group	7A/It 2

| | | | | | | | | **Levels currently at** | | |

Girls	Boys	Roll	SEN SA	SEN SA+	Statement	EAL	G&T	L5/C+	L4/D	L3/G+
6	9	15	4	1	0	1	0	0	11	4

Title: Introduction to ICT – Software	Context: 2 /6

Learning Objectives – WALT (*What we are learning today*)

- Know how to log on and off the computer
- Know why it is important to keep your password secret
- Know what computer software is
- Know how to save files properly

Learning Outcomes – WILF (*What I am looking for*)

- Be able to log on and off the computers in school
- Be able to give examples of software
- Be able to save work in files and folders

1. All should	2. Most should	3. Some should
Be able to log on to the computer to start creating their PowerPoint presentation and know how to save their work.	Be able to competently finish their Facebook sheets and create at least one slide using different fonts and colours.	Be able to create more than one slide on their presentation.

Starter: **Individual paper-based activity** – Display the first slide of *Presentation* and hand out copies of *Worksheet – Own experiences mindmap*. Pupils mindmap their own experiences of using ICT thinking about the different technologies discussed during last lesson.	5 mins

| **Main Activities:**
1. Class discussion – Briefly discuss the use of a username and password to log on to the computer network. Explain to the group that they can use their usernames and passwords to log on to any pupil computer in the school and when they do they should always have access to the user area – this is their individual place to store files. It can only be seen by them and their teachers. | 5 mins |
| **2. Discuss** what pupils had put on their own experiences sheet. Tell pupils that this information may be useful for the task later. Move on to discuss the homework sheets. | 2 mins |

Figure 11.1 Lesson Planning sheet *(continued)*

3. Share objectives with pupils. Explain that last week we talked about computer hardware (ask for examples) and that this week we are interested in software. Demonstrate that by clicking on the Start button, pupils gain access to lots of pieces of software. They should all open Microsoft PowerPoint. Explain that PowerPoint is used to make presentations. Introduce the About Me task by explaining that over the next few weeks they will be creating a presentation about themselves – it will be for other members of the group to get to know a bit about them and so it should be suitable for children aged 11 to 12.	5 mins
4. Hand out the Facebook Sheet which asks pupils to enter information about themselves. Tell pupils that this will form the basis of their presentation, which we will start next.	10 mins
5. Teacher Demonstration – Demonstrate adding a pupil's name to the first slide, then changing background colours, text colour, text size and font. Show how to add a new slide. Hand out help sheet and ensure they use their homework plan.	5 mins
6. Individual activity – Pupils create a new PowerPoint file, this lesson they should focus on the content, possibly including: • **1st Page = Name, Age and Form** • **2nd Page = About Me, Favourite Places to Visit** • **3rd Page = Favourite TV show, Favourite Music** • **4th Page = Favourite/Worst Lesson and Why**	25 mins
Plenary:	
1. Ask a volunteer to demonstrate to the rest of the group how to create and save a new file in a folder using the interactive whiteboard.	2 mins
2. Then ask pupils to save their work into their own folders.	2 mins
Homework (in planners): No homework set.	

Figure 11.1 *(continued)*

of the lesson enables you to set yourself a target. The next thing is how you are going to get there.

Task 11.4

What sort of things should you think about when setting your students a new task?

What do they need to have to enable them to succeed at that task?

The first thing you need to know is what prior learning students have. You have to make sure that your students not only know what they have to do, but that they have a good idea of how to get there. You may have to show them a new skill which needs time. You may need to bring them back for discussions at various points in the lesson. You need to be clear about this because this is what is going to influence the plan itself.

Therefore, the first thing to document once you have clarified this in your mind is the objective or objectives of the lesson. You will be sharing this with your class at the start of the lesson, so it is important that you document this in student-friendly language for when you share it with your class. If you have multiple objectives, keep them short and sharp and small in number. Avoid having more than three objectives if possible. Any more than this and you are risking the students not being able to remember what they are and the focus of the lesson will be too broad.

All, most, some

So, you have established what you want to teach and where you want your students to be by the end of the lesson. The next thing you need to consider is the differentiation realities of your class. It is reasonable to assume that not all students will progress at the same pace and not all students will have the same level of understanding. But it is important to establish where you need to get all of your students to by the end of the lesson. I recommend that you should go with an 'all, most, some' approach for your plan and document it as such. 'All' is the baseline for success of the lesson and the majority of the students (most) should be able to push forward to your next objective. Some will be for the more able students who can take themselves one step further. This is also important for the breakout points which I will deal with later in this chapter. The importance of reaching the 'All' students point is that this will mean you to have reached a place where the following lesson can take place.

The way that you present these objectives and outcomes to the students is important. It needs to be in student-friendly language. In the example lesson plan in Figure 11.1, these are demonstrated as WALT and WILF. Walt can be remembered as 'What we Are Learning Today' and represents the lesson objectives. WILF can be remembered as 'What I am Looking For' and these are the learning outcomes for the lesson. Stating them as WALT and WILF makes them more accessible to the students.

Linking the lesson to the structure

Once you have established your objectives and the basic differentiation in terms of where you expect the students to be at the end of the lesson, the next stage is to link your plan with the lesson itself. It would be fair to say that most lesson plans presume that there is no movement between lessons and that one starts immediately after the other finishes. Obviously, this is not the case, especially if you are teaching in a secondary school where the class may come together from a number of different locations. In some schools, the students will arrive and line up outside the lesson and the teacher lets them in when they are ready, possibly taking the opportunity to check uniform, and so forth. In some schools, health and safety issues such as the width of corridors and the space available for the students mean that the students will be expected to come straight into your lesson. If this is the case, and the students have had to come from different locations, it can result in a straggly start to the lesson with students arriving over a period of a couple of minutes. If this is the reality of your situation, you must plan for it and have some pre-starter activity for the students to arrive to as a part of the routine for the class. This will give the students who have arrived something constructive to do before the remainder of the class arrives.

Whatever the reality is for you, the first activity that you will need to undertake will be a starter. The function of a starter can be varied, ranging from a calming exercise through to checking the understanding of the previous lesson to an activity which will be used later on in the lesson. Whatever you are doing, the starter should be seen as a key part of setting the scene and tone for the lesson. If the starter activity does not involve you directly in an interactive manner, then this could also be a good time to take the register.

From this point you should be introducing your objectives, explaining what it is that you will be doing during the lesson and possibly demonstrating a skill which you expect the students to perform. The basic structure of a lesson would indicate that you are expected to have a starter, a main activity and a summative plenary. This would therefore make your plan very limited indeed. In reality, your lesson should be divided into a series of short activities, punctuated by mini-plenaries which can be used to check understanding, demonstrate good practice, share ideas and set the time for the next activity. This implies an important part of the plan: an awareness of the time that tasks will take. Consequently, when you are planning a lesson, you should be stating the time that each task should take, and when you introduce a task to the students, you should share this time with them. The students will be much more focused if you tell them that they have x minutes to a task than if you set them off with no target to reach. Towards the end of the lesson, you will want to conduct a summative plenary to review the objectives, set the scene for the next lesson and check the learning that has taken place.

The Connect, activate, demonstrate, consolidate model

In this chapter, there are a number of different lesson plans which reflect this structure. There is a good chance that you will experience a number of alternative layouts during your teaching career. One school which I have worked with has developed a plan which I feel works well for trainees. It breaks the lesson into four sections of connect, activate, demonstrate and consolidate (see Figure 11.2). The connect section includes the starter activity, the learning objectives and outcomes as well as the success criteria. It is also in this part of the lesson that the big picture is explained, linking back to the previous lesson. In the activate section, the instructions for the lesson or part of the lesson are given. The demonstrate section is where the students are active in their own

YEAR: 9/10	MODULE: ONU1

LESSON: 21 – Business Letter

STAFF: RTL

KEY WORDS: Letter, date, letterhead, subject, body, recipient details, salutation, signature

Connect Starter, Big picture, learning objectives, learning outcomes and success criteria.

Starter	*10mins* – Students to make corrections to a prewritten letter.
	<5mins – Question and answer format of letter.

ENSURE ROOM STRAIGHT AND TIDY AND DISMISS

Big Picture	Students are working towards completing Unit1 OCR Nationals.
	Students are currently working towards AO4 – creating a range of business documents.
	Previously: AO4 – Theory & Practice of Business docs.
	Next time: AO4 – Business card

Learning Objectives	Understand the correct layout of a letter.
	Understand the appropriate writing style and tone for a letter.
	Understand how to appropriately format a letter.

Learning Outcomes/ Success Criteria	**ALL** – will have written a business letter with formatting.
	MOST – will have spell checked their letter.
	SOME – will have made improvements to the layout/format.

Activate

Teaching Strategies: e.g. Interactive whole class or small group, direct instruction.

1. *<5mins* – Recap on the format of a business letter using boardworks and starter letter and student direction – students to explain formatting features used. **Use keywords!!**

Introduce to letter section of workbook – point out questions to be answered (ppt).

3. *5mins* – Pick up on questions to ensure correctly identified (Who is the audience? What information should it contain? Is it formal or informal?) Explain task and required evidence.

Demonstrate

Learning activities which show learning has taken place, opportunities to apply learning

2. *<5mins* – Students to look through 'Business Letter' section of the work book.

4. *20–25mins* – Students to write their Business letter to students about the Stu Soc trip that they are organising.

Stop point where appropriate: Students must spell check and evidence. (Explain to leave mistakes to the end to show this)

Demonstrate!!

Consolidate Review, reflect, recall what has been learned

Figure 11.2 The connect, activate, demonstrate, consolidate model

learning, demonstrating their understanding. In the consolidate section, plenary activities take place such as reviewing learning. It is clear that this cycle of four events can happen once within a lesson, or many times. However, I feel that it is a good model to work towards when you are planning.

Whatever plan you use during your practice, all parts of the lesson have to be planned and written down in sufficient detail so that you are clear about what you are doing and when, as well as what the students are doing. You should therefore expect your plans to take a considerable amount of your time. However you will find that you become more efficient at planning as your practice develops, even though the amount of time that you spend planning may well remain the same, as your teaching load will increase as your progress through your training.

Using breakout points

One of the most difficult things to do as a trainee teacher is to gauge the length of the lesson and the number of activities which can be expected to be completed within that lesson. As I have indicated earlier in this chapter there is a tendency, especially at the start of the teaching practice, for trainees to overestimate the amount of tasks which can be achieved or underestimate the amount of time it will take to complete a task. Sometimes a trainee can also try to cram too much into a lesson and, as a result, overload their students, resulting in them not learning a great deal effectively. An inexperienced teacher can also try to start a task too late in the lesson and leave the students stranded part-way between. Although there are circumstances when this does happen, it is better to avoid it wherever possible.

We have already established that it is good practice to chunk lessons up into time-defined sessions where the students are on a task and then bought back for a mini-plenary before the next task is started. The fact that you have inserted this structure into your lesson gives you the opportunity to have breakout points within it. A breakout point is that part in the lesson which must be reached but could effectively be identified as the end of the lesson. The breakout point is a very useful tool in that it allows you to build in a certain flexibility to your lesson plan.

Task 11.5

Look at the following scenario:

You are teaching a citizenship lesson on human rights. You have planned for an hour-long lesson, but a debate which you had planned for five or ten minutes had developed further than you had intended or expected. The students are engaged and active, real learning is going on. What would you do?

The big question is, should you stop the discussion when it is going so well? The whole class is active, you are getting good points from the students and you may have some students who do not normally communicate effectively participating in the class.

A good trainee should be able to plan well. A very good trainee should be able to think on their feet and be brave enough to adjust their lesson if being flexible makes for a better lesson.

(MW, Mentor, Minsworth, 2010)

From this quote, it is clear that the mentor values the fact that the trainee can judge a situation well and react to it.

What you could therefore do in this situation is re-evaluate your plan at the time and decide to extend this activity and readjust the other activities. This may mean that some of the activities and objectives are moved to the next session, especially if this means that by expanding one task means that you cover the other sections in more detail and with a stronger level of understanding.

The ability to make active use of breakout points is a skill that can be used by the confident trainee and the experienced teacher. However, I feel that it is important to plan such areas in the lesson plan in case such a situation arises. As you can see from the third lesson plan example (Figure 11.3), a breakout point has been identified in an ICT lesson. In this example, the trainee has identified a possible point where further explanation may occur or the skills practised may take more time than is initially expected. The decision has been made that, if the students get to this point, it may well be worth extending the activity to ensure that learning has not only taken place, but is likely to be retained in subsequent lessons. If you do have a plan which includes breakout points, you should also make sure that you have appropriate extension activities for those students who reach this point early.

In this example (Figure 11.3), the teacher has foreseen that the activity of understanding what constitutes good and poor design points in a website may take longer than expected and has indicated that a breakout point could be inserted before the students go on to discuss issues of validity and bias within design. A second breakout point has been inserted by the teacher after the next milestone activity has been realized. By using this approach, the teacher has built in some flexibility to the lesson plan, should it be needed.

DATE:	CLASS: Y8	UNIT/ MODULE:	No. OF STUDENTS: 28	NO. OF SEN: 4	LESSON OF: 1 of 4	TIME
How does this lesson follow on from the last lesson? **By the end of the lesson what specifically will all/ most/some have learned?**	<td colspan="6">**Connection between this lesson and previous learning** New Subject, but students will have experience of web sites.</td>
	<td colspan="4">**Learning Objectives**</td>	**NC/GCSE Level range**	
	<td colspan="4">**ALL:** at the end of the lesson all of the students should be able to identify basic good and bad design points of a website.</td>		
	<td colspan="4">**MOST:** As above, plus also be able to understand the idea of valid data and the impact of bias in website content.</td>		
	<td colspan="4">**SOME:** As above, but also be able to understand the impact of not having these features.</td>		
How will you engage the students at the beginning of the lesson?	<td colspan="5">**Starter activity** Ask students to enter classroom and hand them starter sheets with spider diagrams relating to good and badly designed websites. Once settled ask students to briefly fill in the sheet. The children will then be asked to help the teacher fill in the spider diagram on the white board from the ideas they wrote from their starter sheets.</td>	10 mins
Variety of activities to support learning preferences?	<td colspan="5">**Learning activities** Students are to turn off their monitors and face the front. The teacher will then use a PowerPoint resource that will give points on what will make good and bad website design.</td>	10 mins
	<td colspan="5">Students will be given a worksheet that will give them websites to visit on their computers. The students will have to follow the instructions on the worksheet and answer questions about good and bad web design. SEN students will be given a more simple worksheet to work through, and G&T students, an extended worksheet. BREAKOUT POINT 1</td>	10 mins
	<td colspan="5">The teacher will then use a PowerPoint resource to explain to the class about validity and bias on websites. BREAKOUT POINT 2</td>	10 mins
	<td colspan="5">Students will be given another worksheet, that will focus on the same three websites that were given in task 1. This time the students will look at the validity of the data and bias and complete the worksheet questions. SEN students will be given a more simple worksheet to work through, and G&T students, an extended worksheet.</td>	15 mins
How will the lesson be anchored and progress in learning shown?	<td colspan="5">**Plenary** Class activity, teacher will hand out 'do' and 'don't' cards to each student. The teacher will then read out a brief list of statements and the students must decide if when designing a website they should do what the statement is suggesting by raising the correct card in the air.</td>	5 mins

Figure 11.3 Lesson plan with breakout points *(continued)*

How will you assess student learning in this lesson?	**Assessment Strategies** Q&A during starter and plenary. Target questioning on specific students. Marking of worksheets		
What are the key words for the lesson?	**Key Words**		**Homework** For next week, students will design a website on a subject taken from a list presented to them.
Who will need support/ extending to make appropriate progress?	**Support Strategies – SEN** Two SEN students with reading difficulties. Simpler worksheets will be provided to accommodate these students.		**Extension Strategies – G&T** Four students classed as G&T. For the first task, students will be given the second task worksheet to look through. For the second task, G&T students will be given an extension worksheet.
Which skills will be used in this lesson	**Skill Mapping**		
	Reading Writing Problem Solving Speaking/Listening	Use of numbers Graphical Skills Working with others Information Seeking	ICT Independent Study Drafting Improving performance
What questions must be asked of students to ensure that gains in learning are being made?	**Key Questions**		

Figure 11.3 *(continued)*

Evaluation

As we have seen, the lesson plan is a more complex thing than a simple indication of the flow of the lesson. If this were the case, you could probably produce one lesson plan and never have to alter it. One of the major driving forces in effective planning is a good understanding of the class you are teaching and the different needs of the group. We have also identified that there are various stages within the lesson which act as milestones within the lesson. It is not enough just to have a starter, main and plenary session on the plan; the lesson needs to be broken down into further sections. We have also seen that the use of breakout points within the lesson can help us work in distinct chunks and avoid a situation where a lesson gets stuck between two points making it more difficult to pick up from there in the next lesson.

A further important aspect of planning is your own evaluation of the success of the lesson which you have just delivered. When doing your evaluation, certain points may naturally stand out. There may be issues with the timing if, for example, a task set needed more or less time than you thought. The pitch of the lesson may have been too high or low or there may be issues with some group work which you did, which has then impacted on classroom dynamics. All of these things will have to be reviewed before you start to plan your next lesson so that you can take these factors into consideration. This form of reflection and personal evaluation of your performance is also a requirement of the QTS Standards and you are required to produce evidence of evaluation for every lesson that you plan for and deliver (Q29).

The sample lesson plan in Figure 11.4 illustrates some of the key questions that a trainee, or anyone teaching students, should be thinking of when evaluating their lesson. You can choose to evaluate directly on to your lesson plan if you wish. However, I would recommend that you create a document like this one and use it separately for your evaluations.

Give reasons for your observations
Did pupils/students achieve the learning outcomes/objectives for the lesson? What evidence do I have?
What were the strengths of the lesson in terms of my teaching and pupil/student learning?
How successful were the Differentiation Strategies used? (Consider these in terms of more able and less able.)
How would I improve this lesson if I taught it again?
What action should I take to improve my lesson with this group, in terms of my teaching and pupil/student learning, the next time I teach them? (Add these to your PDT section of your next lesson plan for this group.)

Figure 11.4 Plan for lesson evaluation

Where does evaluation fit into the process?

As you can see from Figure 11.5 the role of evaluation is one of the component parts of the preparation and delivery of the lesson. It is a cyclical activity and

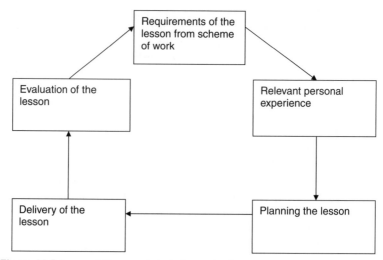

Figure 11.5 Lesson delivery cycle including evaluation

as you can see, the actual delivery of the lesson is a considerable way around the cycle. I would argue that the initial starting point for this process is the requirements of the lesson as governed by the scheme of work, which may in itself be dictated by national specifications and curriculum requirements of the varying exam boards. Into this we would add the personal experiences

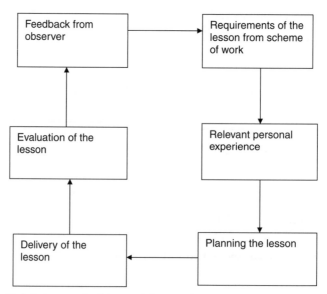

Figure 11.6 Trainee teacher's lesson delivery cycle

of the teacher who will use these to aid in the planning of the lesson. The delivery should therefore reflect the planning, although, as indicated earlier, there may be a need to stray from the plan or adjust it because of the need to implement a breakout point in the exercise. It is also important to note that there is a role for the personal experience of the teacher in terms of their own knowledge which may make the lesson more appealing to the students or the element of experience from years of teaching and awareness of different solutions to different problems.

However, you, as a trainee will not have this sort of experience to draw on and, as a result, need to think about your own evaluation of how things went. At this stage, it is also important to take into the account the comments of those who are observing you as this will be an important source for possible improvements. Therefore, the diagram for the trainee teacher looks more like Figure 11.6.

Summary

In this chapter we have looked at the issue of planning and the implications that it has for you teaching. I hope that it is clear now that the students whom you teach should be at the heart of your planning. Student learning needs to be at the very centre of what you do in your planning. Obviously, there are other factors which are key to this exercise, such as the curriculum you are required to teach and your own personal experiences. Evaluation of your lessons by both you and your mentor are also an important part of the process.

It is clear that planning will take a great deal of your time, especially at the start of your practice but, with experience, you will find that your planning gets better and quicker.

Further reading

Butt, G. (2003) *Lesson Planning*. London: Continuum.
Haynes, A. (2010) *The Complete Guide to Lesson Planning and Preparation*. London: Continuum.
John, P. (2003) *Lesson Planning for Teachers*. London: Cassell.
Skowra, J. (2006) *Powerful Lesson Planning: Every Teacher's Guide to Effective Instruction*. London: Corwin Press.

Useful websites

www.teachernet.gov.uk

www.TeacherNetwork.org

www.teachingideas.co.uk

www.primaryresources.co.uk

12 Assessment of students' work

Contents

- Introduction to assessment
- Formative and summative assessment – what is the difference?
- Assessment for learning
- Assessment for motivation
- How much shall I write?
- The power of verbal motivation
- Working with individuals and small groups
- Self- and peer assessment
- Summary
- Further reading

Learning objectives

In this chapter I will be looking at issues concerning the assessment of students' work. By the end of this chapter your should have a clear understanding of:

- The difference between formative and summative assessment
- The role of assessment for learning in the classroom
- The role of assessment as a motivational tool
- The role of self- and peer evaluation.

QTS Standards

The chapter is particularly relevant to Q Standards 4, 12, 13, 25(c), 25(d), 26(a), 26(b), 27 and 28.

Communicating and working with others

Q4   Communicate effectively with children, young people, colleagues, parents and carers.

Assessment and monitoring

Q12   Know a range of approaches to assessment, including the importance of formative assessment.

Q13   Know how to use local and national statistical information to evaluate the effectiveness of their teaching, to monitor the progress of those they teach and to raise levels of attainment.

Teaching

Q25   Teach lessons and sequences of lessons across the age and ability range for which they are trained in which they:

(c)   adapt their language to suit the learners they teach, introducing new ideas and concepts clearly, and using explanations, questions, discussions and plenaries effectively;

(d)   manage the learning of individuals, groups and whole classes, modifying their teaching to suit the stage of the lesson.

Assessing, monitoring and giving feedback

Q26 (a)   Make effective use of a range of assessment, monitoring and recording strategies.

(b)   Assess the learning needs of those they teach in order to set challenging learning objectives.

Q27   Provide timely, accurate and constructive feedback on learners' attainment, progress and areas for development.

Q28   Support and guide learners to reflect on their learning, identify the progress they have made and identify their emerging learning needs.

Introduction to assessment

The importance of effective assessment is something which has become an increasingly vital part of the teacher's toolkit and a good understanding of assessment is required to meet your standards. Black and Wiliam go as far as to say that assessment is 'at the heart of effective teaching' (Black and Wiliam 1998, p. 2). As a child many years ago my work was marked with a tick or cross using a red pen. Teachers rarely wrote anything in a student's book other than the occasional 'well done', 'poor' or 'see me'. Therefore a student had very little idea of what they had got right, wrong, or completely wrong. There was certainly little or no direction about what may have been wrong and how to put this right, or how to improve their work or indeed how to move it up to the next level. The informative part of assessment was sadly lacking as a role in teaching. However, this is no longer the case with the drive for Assessment for Learning (AfL) behind this empowering change, so that a student today is much more likely to understand what level they are working at and how to improve their work.

Formative and summative assessment – what is the difference?

This may sound a little odd, but there are times when teachers and trainees alike get confused between formative and summative assessment. To set the record straight, summative assessment is the final mark which you will give for a piece of work. In this instance, you will give a grade and usually a comment as to why this grade has been given. The feedback on this piece of work may be used to inform future work, but not the piece of work which has been submitted.

Formative assessment is more informative. It is designed to explain where a piece of work is at a particular time, and more importantly, what is needed to improve the piece of work prior to final submission. It can also be used to gauge a student's level of understanding, as a motivational tool or as a guide to the effectiveness of your teaching, thus impacting on your planning and teaching. Formative assessment can come in many forms but it is basically any activity undertaken by teachers and, importantly, the students themselves, which can be used to inform teaching and learning. As a consequence of this, formative assessment is also frequently referred to as Assessment for Learning.

Task 12.1

Name as many methods as you can to identify the levels of understanding of your students.

What methods would you use to inform your students of the level of their work and how to improve it?

Assessment for learning

As indicated above, formative assessment can take many forms. Hopefully, the days when the teacher sets a task and remains firmly behind their desk until the work is handed in at the end of the lesson have long gone. Thankfully, teaching has become much more interactive. You are expected to ask students what they think, encourage them to vocalize their opinions and ask them to present their work in a variety of ways. This is not to say that all lessons occur in a glitzy world of multimedia presentations. Reality suggests that, for the most part, we will be in a similar teaching environment to when we were taught, the good old classroom where the class enters to work at desks and the teacher closes the door until the end of the lesson. What has changed is the way that we work within that room. No teacher, under any circumstances, should give up on a student just because that student's learning style does not match their teaching style. If you find that you have tried a certain technique time and time again but still a child does not understand, then it is simply time to try a different approach because clearly the one you are using is not working. In today's climate of personalized learning, a teacher has to take much more responsibility for working with each member of that class, not simply the ones who respond well to their teaching style. It is the teacher who needs to change if the student does not understand, not the student.

Assessing for motivation

I feel that one of the obvious but frequently neglected uses of assessment is for motivation. The way we, as teachers, use written assessment in particular is crucial in this aspect. As a student, seeing work marked 'Well Done' or 'Excellent' has a very positive impact on their self-esteem, just as a negative comment has a harmful and arguably destructive impact on a child's self-view. In this section, I will be looking at the do's and don'ts of giving written feedback to a student and the effect that this has upon them.

Task 12.2

What do you understand about the function of giving written assessment on a piece of work?

Does the colour of the ink you use affect the way that a student sees their marks?

The most important thing about written assessment is that it needs to be a continual process, not just an occasional activity. If a student's work is important, and it always is, it needs to be respected and the best way to do this is by giving it your attention and the benefit of your expertise. This action sends a very clear message to the students that you care. A student is much more likely to work for you if they think that it will be marked than if they know it will simply be languishing in a cupboard until the next lesson. You have to make time to invest in this activity. Another important reason for marking as a continual process is the formative nature of this work. It is not good simply marking the work at the end of the task and then drawing the attention of the students to the errors they have made and the way that it could have been improved. It is too late then and can cause some resentment on behalf of the student, especially if they have put a great deal of personal effort into it.

Task 12.3

Scenario

David is a Y10 student producing a piece of work for English. The work is based on a poem which has been read in class. The poem has struck a note with Dave and he is keen to put his ideas on paper. Dave does not usually put a great deal of effort into his work but is proud of what he has completed in class. When you come to work on it that evening, you note that Dave's work has spelling and grammar errors in it and he has missed one of the key points of the poem in his explanation. How do you mark the work?

The first thing to consider with Dave is the investment for the future, which is arguably more important than the single piece of work you are about to mark. Dave is usually disengaged and does not see the relevance of literature; he is more focused on music but this poem has struck a chord with him. So what mark should Dave be awarded? Dave may think that it is an A* piece of work but in reality you may think that it is closer to a C, yet Dave normally submits work of an E standard. This is a tricky situation and a balance needs to be struck. The important thing to note is that, probably for the first time this year, a disengaged and probably underperforming student has engaged. Get this wrong and the student may well withdraw back into his shell. Get it right and you may get a total change of attitude.

I would suggest the following technique would be the most beneficial. First, it is very important to be positive. Never, ever start with a negative comment in your comments at the end of the work. If someone has tried their hardest, the impact of reading 'Disappointing' or 'Poor' as an opening comment can be crushing. It is also likely to ensure that the student will not read further and you will merely affirm a student's negative feelings about their own progress.

If a teacher writes something negative at the start, I do not read anything else he has put. If a teacher writes something positive at the start I would. If it tells me how to improve, I don't mind, so long as they say something encouraging.

(Ahmed A, Y9, Parkwood School)

This comment is further supported by Black and Wiliam who state that:

> Pupils who encounter difficulties and poor results are led to believe that they lack ability, and this belief leads them to attribute their difficulties to a defect in themselves about which they cannot do a great deal. So they 'retire hurt', avoid investing effort in learning which could only lead to disappointment. And will try to build up their self-esteem in other ways.
>
> (Black and Wiliam 1998, p. 9)

Therefore, it is important that you put something positive about the work. The student will then be more likely to read on to see what you are suggesting to help them to improve their work. It is also important to not overload the student with suggestions. You have a better chance of getting a positive response if the student can see that there is a real and achievable task for them to perform. Finally, it is important to acknowledge the progress made after the student has made the changes you have suggested.

This has short- and long-term benefits. First, the quality of the work will be improving to the point where you want it to be. Second, the student is more likely to engage with you if you are positive towards them. Third, as the student's self-esteem rises, they are more likely to implement your suggestions as a matter of course, be more confident in their abilities, and consequently be more willing to push themselves. A student will normally be a more willing contributor to the lesson and be more self-critical of their own work. Finally, and most importantly, you are more likely to have a more contented and constructive student.

I have stressed the importance of giving comments, making them positive as well as informative and avoiding entirely negative comments as demotivational. But what of the grades you have to give? What impact can they have? Black and Wiliam are very clear on this point. They feel that grades by themselves are of little or no benefit to the students without constructive feedback. In fact, they go as far as to question their use at all as an effective way of helping learning.

> Feedback has been shown to improve learning where it gives each pupils specific guidance on strengths and weaknesses, preferably without and overall marks.
>
> (Black and Wiliam 1998, p. 12)

However, the reality of your situation within school may mean that you have to put a grade on the work. It may well be school and department policy and we are expected to share levels with our students. However, the important thing is the way that you present this. If the grade is over-stressed, or worse still, used to rank students within the classroom, it will have a negative effect on those students who do not achieve the top grades and may, in some cases, merely confirm a student's negative belief in their own ability. Therefore, if you do have to give a grade, reduce its status in terms of how you display it to the students and place the emphasis on the feedback, explaining how this piece of work, rather than the grade could be improved.

Having said this, careful use of marks, if shared with the student in a sensitive way, can be used as an effective and motivational tool. You may be in a situation to demonstrate to your student their individual progress by following the advice given in their feedback. Therefore, by showing the student the progress that he/she has made, you may well be in a situation to set further aspirational targets which a student may now have the confidence to strive for.

How much should I write?

Some would say that this is a 'how long is a piece of string?' sort of question. One word is next to useless. If the objective is to pass a comment and explain how to improve, you need to have more than that. You should also avoid writing too much as it will put the student off from reading it plus you may quickly get resentful that you are writing more than your student. I am an advocate of writing no more than you can put on a Postit note. It makes sure that you are succinct and that, after you have put your positive comment, you can only put a few comments for improvement. I have seen this advice taken literally by one of my PGCE students in a school in north Sheffield. When marking the students' work, he wrote on a Post it note and put it with the piece of work. When I discussed it with the students, they were very positive about the technique as they felt that it meant that their work was kept clear of other people's writing (they were clearly proud of their work) and that it gave them enough to act upon. The fact that every piece of work had a Post it note also demonstrated to the students that their teacher cared for what they had done and consequently, they took more care about what they submitted. One argument against this would be that the Post it could get lost, but from what I have seen, the students kept the Post it notes and more importantly, read and acted on them and that, after all, is what we want.

The power of verbal motivation

Task 12.4

Apart from written assessment, what other techniques could you use for formative assessment?

Think about your own classroom practice and identify where you directly or indirectly assess your students' performance.

It should go without saying that a good teacher is assessing the progress of their students all the time and using this knowledge to help them to plan their lessons, direct their questioning and develop activities and resources. A good teacher will make this look easy and it is reasonable to say that experience helps in this department. However, it is important to be aware of the opportunities and implement them into your practice as soon as you are able.

Let's take the starter activity as your first opportunity. There are lots of separate activities that could be undertaken as a starter. First, it is important to establish what you think is the function of your starter activity. It could be a question and answer session or activity to check prior learning. You may be linking back to a previous lesson before introducing new ideas or skills. It could be a calming task to introduce key words or to simply get the students in the right frame of mind for the lesson you are about to deliver. It could be an individual activity or a paired or group activity.

Whatever starter you are doing, it is the first opportunity you will have to assess your students and should not be wasted. Remember, you are looking at creating a positive working environment where a student should feel comfortable to share their ideas. If you are asking questions, your response to the answers they give must be positive and not a put down, no matter what answer your students give. At first, you may well get the class clown giving you a silly answer but if you handle this well and show that you value students' comments, the class clown will be less likely to try to derail you in the future.

If you are asking questions, you are also in a position to direct the appropriate question to the right student. If a student is nervous or unwilling to answer a question, make sure you ask them one where they can get the answer right and make sure they get lots of praise for it. This investment will be worth it because it will make the less confident student more likely to answer again if they feel safe to do it. If you were in a situation where you lacked confidence and you finally plucked up the courage to voice an opinion, would you be likely to put yourself forward again if you had been put down by the teacher on a previous occasion? It is important to avoid the temptation of asking answers from the same students who put their hands up again and again. You may establish what Keen Kevin knows but not the other members of the class. You may wish to ask a question and have a 'no hands up' policy saying that you will give the students a few seconds to think of an answer, by themselves or with a partner, and then you will pick someone to answer yourself, thus ensuring that all take part. Remember, it is important to spread your questions around your class and not to favour a small group of students who you know will give you the right answer.

Working with individuals and small groups

As indicated earlier in this section, there will be some students who will be unwilling to put themselves forward when answering questions, especially in front of the whole class. However, you will not be in a situation where there are whole class questions all of the time and there will be lots of opportunities for working with small groups and individuals. If you do this part well, you may also raise the self-esteem of individuals which should result in them being more willing to participate in the whole class questioning which tends to be part of starter activities and whole class plenaries.

If your class has been set a timed groupwork activity, this should allow you the time to move between the groups, prompting questions and checking which students are being active and which ones are not and ensuring that individuals do not dominate groups. Obviously, part of the skill of effective group work is selecting the size and make-up of the group. The easy technique is to allow students to work in friendship groups. If this works, then fine. But the danger is that friends remain sociable within their group, which may impact on the amount of work they do. I would suggest that a more effective technique is to engineer the make-up of the group, selecting individuals who may work together but who would not normally, or making sure that those whose voice may not be normally heard get a chance to put their views across. You may also choose to mix genders, abilities and known opinions. What you should always avoid is getting all of the same type of student in the same group. For example, if you allow all of the high achieving girls or boys in one group together, then they may still continue to dominate the class with their answers. The students who are less confident or articulate may well withdraw and not be willing to contribute to their lesson for fear of getting the answers wrong.

Group activities usually result in a feedback to the class of the findings of the group. How the feedback is delivered is also important. A skilled teacher will always target their questions appropriately. You may elect a spokesperson for the group. However, this may result in one person dominating and the rest sitting back. My suggestion is to target questions within the group itself and not to the group as a whole. Thus you can ensure that the group has worked as a team and no one has been left out as everyone is expected to be able to answer.

The most important assessment, however, is not of the class or of the group but of the individual. Working as a pair or a group may help to formulate ideas but it is how the individual understands and articulates what they have learnt that is key. The traditional way to check this understanding has been through the summative mark given to a piece of work handed to the teacher at the end of the exercise. This is then graded, given a comment and handed back. But what is the individual to do with it then? Unless there is a way to implement the feedback, how can they improve? As I have already said in this section, the use of positives when marking a student's work is key to their self-esteem and progress. So too is the activity of the individual formative assessment given by the teacher when talking to their students on a one-to-one basis and inputting into their work before it is submitted, offering suggestions and encouragement, clarifying uncertainties and giving directions. It is no use telling a student that their work is wrong and walking away from them, leaving them feeling humiliated and hostile, it is all about helping them to see how to improve and setting appropriate and achievable targets. The most effective way to do this is simply taking the opportunity to talk to individuals as they are working. Check that they understand what they are doing, ask those questions you want to have answered, point the student in the direction you wish them to go in.

Self- and peer assessment

In this section, I will look at self-assessment and peer assessment and its importance in learning. This is increasingly being used in the classroom and, when done well, is effective in allowing a student to identify good points and areas for development. It does not replace the teacher's role in assessment; they should be able to identify targets at a higher level than their students. Self-assessment gives a student the chance to step back and look at their own work and set their own targets. However, it is vital that students are given a framework to work within. It is not enough to say 'What do you think of your work?' as you may only get the answer 'Fine', which tells no one anything. Create a framework where the student can assess their work. This may be in the form of a check list to identify if a student has performed a task and then give a space for their own recommendations of how to improve their work. You could also differentiate the assessment sheet by making suggestions as to what the student could do to improve their work. This exercise is only meaningful if the student then has the opportunity to implement their suggestions.

Peer assessment is also a very popular way to look at individuals' work. This could be done as a paired activity where work is simply swapped between two students and an assessment conducted. If you are lucky enough to possess an interactive whiteboard and your students have been working on a network, you may be able to display a student's work to the whole class. Some may see this as a high risk strategy; however, it depends on the atmosphere you have created in the class itself. If you have managed to create an atmosphere where students feel confident in sharing their work, or at least comfortable enough to feel that their work will not be ridiculed, then this technique can be very successful. I would suggest the following technique. First, explain what you are about to do. Second, identify all the positives about the piece of work. Next, engage the students whose work it is to explain an aspect about the work and be positive about what they have said and drawn attention to. Then ask individuals what they think. The important thing is to make the experience a positive one. This should never be used to ridicule a piece of work in front of the whole class.

This is an excellent way of identifying and sharing good practice, raising a student's self-esteem and creating a positive classroom atmosphere. After the first few times of this technique being used, I can guarantee that most students will see displaying their work as a positive thing and may well ask for their work to be displayed.

Summary

In this section I have looked at issues surrounding assessing students' work. I have clarified the difference between formative and summative assessment. I have identified the importance of being positive and constructive in the areas of feedback and the equal importance of avoiding negative comments. I have also considered the role played by questioning in assessment and the importance of self- and peer evaluation as an empowering activity. The most important thing to remember about assessment is that it should be informative and offer advice about how to improve the piece of work that your student is currently working on. It should also be used as a tool to raise self-esteem to ensure future productivity and the confidence of the student whose work is being assessed.

Further reading

Black, P. and Wiliam, D. (1998) *Inside the Black Box*. London: Nfer Nelson.
Black, P. and Wiliam, D. (2002) *Working Inside the Black Box*. London: Nfer Nelson.
Black, P. et al. (2003) *Assessment for Learning: Putting it into Practice*. Maidenhead: McGraw-Hill.
Brooks, V. (2002) *Assessment in Secondary Schools*. Maidenhead: McGraw-Hill.
Fautley, M. and Savage, J. (2008) *Assessment for Learning and Teaching in Secondary Schools*. Exeter: Learning Matters.

13 | Teaching and learning using ICT

Contents

- Introduction to ICT in the classroom
- Planning to use ICT in your lesson
- Restricting choice – use of the internet in the classroom
- Classroom management in an ICT suite
- The use of virtual learning environments (VLEs) in schools
- Summary
- Further reading

Learning objectives

By the end of this chapter, you should have better understanding of:

- The general use of the ICT as a teaching and learning aid
- The advantages and disadvantages of the use of the internet in the classroom
- Issues of classroom management in ICT
- The role of the VLE in education.

QTS Standards

This chapter is particularly relevant to QTS Standards 8, 14, 17, 23 and 24.

Personal and professional development

Q8 Have a creative and constructively critical approach towards innovation, being prepared to adapt their practice where benefits and improvements are identified.

Subjects and curriculum

Q14 Have a secure knowledge and understanding of their subjects/curriculum areas and related pedagogy to enable them to teach effectively across the age and ability range for which they are trained.

Literacy, numeracy and ICT

Q17 Know how to use skills in literacy, numeracy and ICT to support their teaching and wider professional activities.

Planning

Q23 Design opportunities for learners to develop their literacy, numeracy and ICT skills.

Q24 Plan homework or other out-of-class work to sustain learners' progress and to extend and consolidate their learning.

Introduction to ICT in the classroom

In this chapter, I will be looking at the use of ICT in the classroom and expand this out to the wider use of virtual learning environments (VLEs). The use of ICT is key to all areas of the curriculum and is included as a requirement for all subjects. Effective teaching using ICT is a considerable skill and one which is frequently misunderstood. As an ICT teacher myself, I was infuriated by the all too common comments based on the assumption that teaching ICT is easy because the students are interested in what you are doing. Wrong. What you spend a great deal of time doing within ICT is making sure that the students are doing what you want them to do, and not what they want to do, which is basically try to play games, use social networking sites or do some form of research. The arrival of Prom Night from the USA as a rite of passage for year 11s causes considerable disruption at a time when students should be finishing off course work prior to their April/May deadlines. Basically, using ICT has a different style of pedagogy to a number of other subjects. Obviously, being hands on, it tends to benefit those students who prefer a more kinaesthetic style of learning. However, there are a number of handy hints and tips for the use of ICT equipment which will be useful to any trainee teacher. It is also vital that you get to grips with ICT facilities and their use in the classroom as you are required to evidence them as part of your QTS Standards.

Planning to use ICT in your lesson

The use of ICT equipment is not quite as novel as it once was. However, there are a number of things to consider before you use it in your lessons. First, what are you using it for? Are you using ICT to find out or present or both? Are you using it to gather information such as a data in a science lab, for example, or trying to find out about the American West in a history lesson? There are many horror stories about people going into a computer lab and giving students a lack of direction as to what they need to be looking for and what they should be producing. The internet gives access to all sorts of harmful information as well as the useful things you want the students to look at. Preparation is therefore vital to a successful session and the best lessons using ICT have a considerable element of work done away from computers.

The first thing to consider is the task itself. What exactly do you want to do? Are you going to do research on the life and times of William Shakespeare, look into the rings of Saturn or consider issues of personal health such as drugs education? Once you are clear what you want, you need to pull together a clear exercise or set of instructions for the students to follow. Letting students have open access to research may be good for some children but it does require a considerable maturity which some students will possess and many will not. To this end, I would always recommend a session before you use ICT equipment which sets the scene for what is needed for the task and identify where your students could get the information from. The best way to avoid chaos and confusion in an ICT session is to make sure that the students know exactly what they have to do and what sites they have to use to find the data.

Restricting choice – use of the internet in the classroom

Task 13.1

Do you think that all students should have open access to the internet to support the curious mind and promote independent learning?

One of the principal benefits and bonuses of using the internet is the huge amount of resources available to you. As most school children tend not to approach their studies in the same way as an adult learner, the more structure you have to a lesson the better. Obviously, most schools operate a network which already has content filters to remove the worst offending sites but it is still important that you check the sites you want the students to use if an internet session is intended. You want to check for both the content of the sites plus its ability to run on your network. I have seen many planned sessions which have fallen foul of the fact that the students cannot access the sites which the teacher expected them to be able to use because the teacher had access at home. Assume nothing is the safest bet. Check the content and the access rights which may well be different for students and staff. The best thing to do would be to check with a member of the teaching staff responsible for the delivery of ICT in the school, or failing that, ask the network manager/technicians.

Once you have decided which sites you want to use and why, the next question has to be, how do the students access the relevant URL? You could tell the students, but they will forget it and or misspell it resulting in you going round the class taking valuable time making sure that the correct URL is entered. You could put it in the 'favourites' section if the students have the ability to access it. You may write it on the board and get the students to copy it in. However, the best and most secure method I have seen in terms of making sure the students access the right location with the minimum of fuss is to include the site address on an online worksheet, which simply requires the student to click onto the address in the text to be taken to the right location. Again, this will mean some preparation on your part in as much as you will have to get a worksheet together and on a place in the network where the students can get to it, but it is worth the effort.

Classroom management in an ICT suite

As indicated earlier, a common misconception is that students are more engaged if they are using ICT equipment and, as a consequence, will be more focused and productive. Those of us who teach regularly in ICT suites are aware of how difficult this can be and may well scoff at those whose misguided comments come home to roost when they enter an ICT room and see their carefully planned lesson crumble due to their inability to control hardware, software, connection speeds, or passwords as well as the students themselves. They may well like to use ICT equipment but not necessarily for the reasons you want them to! You are also using facilities where the students may well know considerably more than you do and have their own expectations of the functionality of the network due to home ownership.

So, how do you control an ICT suite? The first thing you need to know about is the ability of the network to do what you want it to do. Many schools have fast networks but these are often a few years behind the current technology that you and your students are used to at home. You may not have collaborative use on the network because e-mails are restricted due to the potential negative impact on learning as well as the possibility of cyber bullying. The use of data sticks may well be banned to reduce the threat of viruses, so if you want students to continue working from home, think about how they can access it. Does your school run a VLE and, if so, do the students know how to use it?

As you can see, there are a great many things to think about before you get into the room. But what about the room? What is the layout? How will this impact on your ability to teach? Most schools have hardwired computer facilities so this restricts the way that you can work within a computer suite. It is a reasonable expectation that you should be able to go into a computer suite to find 30 functioning machines in the room, however, there may be more or less. But the overall assumption is that there should be one machine per student, although there may be times when this is not the case. However, I will assume that there are machines for all for the sake of this chapter.

The layout of the room has a huge impact on how you teach in it. A traditional classroom tends to have the students more or less facing the teacher which could be in rows, in groups of tables, in a square, and so forth. This may not be the case in an ICT room where power supplies, access to network points and hubs and physical space all play a part. You may well have a situation where all of the machines face away from the teacher, with the result that all of the students have their backs to you when working, although you have the advantage of being able to see their screens to check that they are working the way you want them to. If the students are all facing you, then their machines will not be, so how do you know what they are doing? Some rooms have simply evolved from other uses and so machines are scattered around the room. In new builds, purpose-built suites have been created although it would be reasonable to say that some of the designs reflect a good look rather than effective use.

I would appear to be painting a pretty bleak picture of the use of the ICT suite. However, this is more about making you think about the facilities you have available to you and pointing out some of the pitfalls of simply walking into a computer suite and expecting everything to be easy. It is not. So here are some suggestions about how to reduce those pitfalls and focus the students on task. The first and most obvious thing to do is to make the lesson as well planned and interesting as possible. Be clear about your aims and what you expect the students to produce in the lesson and why. Second, prepare your own resources well in advance and check that the school's network will allow you to teach the lesson you want to deliver. If you want to demonstrate a skill to the students, make sure that you know how to do it.

When you go into a computer suite, it is as important to treat it in the same way as you would any practical subject. There are more opportunities for health and safety issues in an ICT suite than there are in a standard classroom, for example. Therefore, movement inside an ICT suite needs to be calm and controlled. Consequently, you need to meet your students at the door to ensure a calm and controlled start to the lesson. If your class has a separate area with desks away from the computers, get the students to sit there first before they go to the computers. Remember, a seating plan is just as important in an ICT suite as it would be in a normal classroom, so you decide where people sit. I suggest that you number the machines and allocate the students to them. It may take a little time, but it is worth the investment, especially if you intend to use the room over a number of weeks.

The next thing to remember is that the students are going to be using hardware and software which is much more interesting than you and the last thing you want to do is to find yourself talking to yourself. There are two main ways of controlling the class at this point. One simple technique which is very effective is to simply insist that the monitors are switched off when you are talking to the students and you can check this by walking around the room rather than remaining static on one location. If this is built into the class routine, then it is very effective. A second option depends upon the functionality of your school's network. An increasing number of school networks have network control software. This software allows you to monitor the activity of the machines within a room. Consequently, this allows you to send messages to the whole class or individual machines, take control of machines, share screens and lock and unlock activity on particular machines on the network. This obviously is a very powerful piece of software, both easy to use and great for keeping an eye on what your students are doing at any point. It also has the benefits of being able to capture an individual student's work and share it with the class to demonstrate good practice for example. It is also very handy for a situation where you may want to introduce a new skill or new scenario to extend the set task, for example.

So far I have discussed the importance of the task itself, control within the classroom and the use of software to facilitate the task you wish the students to perform. It is also very important to be very visible within the classroom, moving around the class and encouraging the students, clarifying any queries and providing assessment in all of its varying forms.

The end of the lesson also needs to be very controlled. Getting to the point where the bell goes before telling the students to log off is not the best use of time. The effective use of a summative plenary is as important in a lesson using ICT facilities as it is any other lesson, so make sure you provide the time for this, especially if you intend to use the final few minutes to demonstrate student's work for peer evaluation and identification of good practice. As with any lesson, you should make sure that the students understand what is required of them in the next session.

The use of virtual learning environments (VLEs) in schools

The use of Virtual Learning Environments (VLEs) and Managed Learning Environments (MLEs) is an increasingly important feature of education in the twenty-first century. The ability of each child in a secondary school to be able to access a VLE by 2010 was a clear target set by the Labour Government at the turn of the century. This does not, however, mean that they are widely used by all subjects at the present moment and access to and use by schools will vary from institution to institution. The cost of implementing a VLE also means that, at the moment, their use is very limited in primary education.

The principle is a relatively simple one although the educational implications are huge. The VLE becomes the principal means of access for the students when they log on to their school network. When the students log on, they will typically have access to a work area for each subject, an e-mail account and an area for announcements, reminders from school, etc. If a teacher wishes to put work onto the network, they can place in the appropriate area for their students. Depending on the VLE in question, the teacher may have the facility to set the piece of work to individuals, or set up small groups who can work collaboratively on a piece of work. The teacher may also wish to set deadlines for work. The students may then post their work online to the teacher and receive feedback in the same way. One of the main advantages of this development is that it allows students to continue with their work outside normal school hours, assuming they have access to the internet. It also means that parents can see exactly what online work their children are doing at school.

It is important to note that VLEs are not a replacement for the teacher but simply a different and more up-to-date method of receiving and submitting work and, more importantly, one which your students are more likely to feel comfortable with.

Task 13.2

What effect do you think that the widespread use of VLEs will have on the working life of

a. The students?

b. The teachers?

Summary

In this chapter we have looked at some of the issues concerning the use of ICT facilities in the classroom, from resource development to classroom management.

One of the key things to understand when using ICT facilities is that it represents a different pedagogical approach from the 'normal' classroom and that the main issue is not necessarily student engagement but engagement in the right thing. A good ICT teacher can make this process easy; however, the opportunities offered with ICT, especially the internet, can make teaching a difficult experience unless you manage to make your task interesting and accessible. Consequently, careful planning is your key to success in this area.

A second key point from this chapter is the use of VLEs both within and outside school. If VLEs are embraced and used effectively then they offer a huge range of possibilities for the teacher and the student.

Further reading

Gillespie, H. et al. (2007) *Learning and Teaching with Virtual Learning Environments.* Exeter: Learning Matters.

Kennewell, S. (2004) *Meeting the Standards Using ICT for Secondary Schools*. London: RoutledgeFalmer.

Leask, M. (2000) *Issues in Teaching Using ICT*. London: Routledge.

Leask, M. and Pachler, N. (2005) *Learning to Teach Using ICT in the Secondary School*. London: Routledge.

Russel, T. (2001) *Teaching and Learning Using ICT in Secondary Schools*. London: David Fulton.

Sutherland, R. et al. (2009) *Improving Classroom Learning with ICT*. London: Routledge.

Woollard, J. (2007) *Learning and Teaching Using ICT for Secondary Teaching*. Exeter: Learning Matters.

14 Coping with assignments

Contents

- Issues with assignments – an introduction
- School-based tasks
- Written assignments
- Summary

Learning objectives

In this chapter we discuss issues concerning:

- The differing nature of assignments
- The difference between school-based tasks and university coursework
- The importance of time management when producing assignments on a professional course.

QTS Standards

This chapter is particularly relevant to QTS Standards 7(a), 10, 11 and 15.

Personal and professional development

Q7 (a)   Reflect on and improve their practice, and take responsibility for identifying.

Teaching and learning

Q10   Have a knowledge and understanding of a range of teaching, learning and behaviour management strategies and know how to use and adapt them, including how to personalise learning and provide opportunities for all learners to achieve their potential.

Assessment and monitoring

Q11 Know the assessment requirements and arrangements for the subjects/curriculum areas in the age ranges they are trained to teach, including those relating to public examinations and qualifications.

Subjects and curriculum

Q15 Know and understand the relevant statutory and non-statutory curricula, frameworks, including those provided through the National Strategies, for their subjects/curriculum areas, and other relevant initiatives applicable to the age and ability range for which they are trained.

Issues with assignments – an introduction

In my experience, the main problems which trainees have with assignments arises from time management issues. A common complaint is, how can I do assignments, preparation and marking and teaching at the same time? Surely, something has to give? There may also be added home pressures, especially if you have children of your own to look after. This may mean that you cannot start any of these activities until your children are in bed and this can put a great strain on trainee teachers. The issue therefore becomes one of time management and prioritizing, which is not an easy thing to do. However, you do have to do all of these things, so you will have to find a way through. Refer back to Chapter 6 for more help on time management.

The time you have available will obviously depend on the stage at which you are in your course and your teaching practice. The earlier on in your placement you are, the less teaching time you will have and, arguably, the less will be expected of you in terms of what you have to provide, although you may not see this at the time. If you are at the start of your first teaching placement, your mentor may reasonably expect you to have covered aspects of planning at university, but will be looking to add and develop that skill while on placement. On your second teaching placement, it would be reasonable for your mentor to expect you to have a good grasp of planning and simply expect you to adjust to the planning style of that school. Basically, your work load and the expectations of the school will expand as your practice continues. Therefore, it is a good idea to frontload and get your assignments out of the way as soon as possible.

School-based tasks

The assessment of school-based tasks is something which varies from institution to institution. In some institutions where these tasks are not formally assessed, some unwise trainees will avoid engaging with them since they perceive them as unimportant. This is not the case! Even if they are not formally assessed, the data you gather may well be useful for evidencing standards, providing the base for other assignments or may simply help you to get a good feel for the school that you are at in terms of the staff and the students.

On your first placement, you are likely to be given a group of activities to help you settle in to your school. A typical example of this sort of task is given, taken from the PGCE ICT course at Sheffield Hallam University. You will see that there is a considerable amount of activity which requires the trainee to find information about the courses delivered, the staffing and resources available, as well as undertaking observations with a list of questions to focus the observer on the activity in the classroom. The observation list in particular is very long but designed to make you think about all of the activities which are going on in the classroom, which an experienced teacher does as a matter of course.

Example of School-Based Tasks

Week 1

Outcomes

By the end of the week, you will have

Activity 1

- Noted details about the teaching of your subject including.
- Found out where & when your subject is taught.
- Identified how pupils are assessed.
- Identified what syllabuses are used in the different Key Stages.
- Identified where student work is held.
- Identified the homework policy in your subject.
- Identified how much student work is used in display.
- Identified any subject specific equipment which may exist.

Activity 2

- Observe the teaching of your subject across the different Key Stages.

During the observation note down the following:

Was there a starter, if so, what was it?

What were the objectives of the lesson?

What was the focus of the lesson?

What resources were used – helpsheets, task sheets, etc.?

Was there a plenary, if so, what?

Was there a clear three-part lesson?

Other things to consider about the lesson:

Was there a clear routine? (students line up outside, students log on and then switch the monitors off).

Was there a machine for each student?

Is a seating plan in place?

What is the condition of the room you are in?

At what point was the register called?

Did the teacher use student names?

Did the teacher use questioning, if so, what were they and what type of question was it?

Who answered the questions?

What was the atmosphere like?

How does a Key Stage 3 lesson 'feel' in comparison to a Key Stage 4?

What level of independence does the class demonstrate?

If the lesson is a coursework-based one, what is the role of the teacher?

Did the teacher use student work as an example? What effect do you think this has?

Week 2

Outcomes

By the end of the week you should have:

- observed further lessons

- monitored on/off task activity of at least two pupils

- counted and classify teacher questions during a lesson segment

- examined pupils' work and related it to the National Curriculum levels.

Activity 1

Observe a further two lessons, if possible, use different teachers within your subject and repeat the whole process.

Activity 2

You are also required to perform a task where you will be asked to observe two separate students on separate occasions. Note down the age group, gender, lesson content and general ability of the class.

Closely observe your identified student for 15 minutes and, at the end of each minute, record his/her activity in a table: classify this as on or off task. What are your feelings about what you observe?

Min.	Activity	On	Off	Comment
1				
2				

Activity 3

During a single activity in a lesson, classify all the questions a teacher asks according to open-endedness and level of difficulty: note the response.

Record verbatim those questions you regard as being very open-ended.

Evaluate the session:

- what happens when a hard question is not answered?
- what happens when an open question is answered wrongly?
- what are the purposes of the questions?

Activity 4

Look at some of the work produced by pupils

- What section of the National Curriculum does it mainly fall within?
- What level is the work?
- Is the quality what you had expected, or better, or worse? Why?

Acquire copies of the work which you have been reviewing and write your comments on them.

Week 3

Outcomes

The following tasks will enable you to become familiar with

- your school's approach to planning schemes of work and lessons
- the nature and frequency of assessments and their reporting
- the nature and purpose of project work at KS4.

Activity 1

Collect some examples of schemes of work or lesson plans used by the school.

- How are schemes of work produced and how are lesson plans developed?

- Are they available to you and/or others?

- How are the pupils made aware of the aims and objectives or expected outcomes?

- Who develops the schemes at KS3 and KS4?

Activity 2

How do teachers assess pupils and what are the assessments used for?

- What evidence is there of formative and informal assessment?

- Examine how teachers help pupils in class – what information does this give the teacher, is it recorded, is it used?

- Is assessment used to advise future success, i.e. assessment for learning?

- How is student progress monitored?

- What evidence is there of formative or summative assessment and what forms does it take?

- How and where is assessment recorded and to whom is it reported?

- How are NC levels assessed?

Activity 3

Look at the range of projects undertaken – especially at KS4.

- What sort of projects are undertaken and for what courses/syllabuses?

- What range of topics is there within a class/year group?

- Are the projects for real or realistic end users?

- Do they allow a range of skills to be demonstrated?

- How is quality judged?

- How are the pupils supported at the various stages?

As you can see, these types of tasks require you to be active in issues surrounding observation and assessment and are not only designed to get you used to the way your subject is delivered but also to think critically about the lessons you are observing. As you will also note, the complexity of what you are asked to do expands as the weeks go on. This process is intended to take you to the point when you will start to take over your own lessons and it is intended that you will be able to get a good grasp of the schemes of work, the assessment techniques and the overall norms of the department.

The observation task for the first week is designed to make you look at the lesson from a broader perspective than simply, was it a good lesson or not? Rather it encourages you to think about what makes the lesson up and therefore enables you to see what a complex task teaching actually is. In the second week, you are expected to expand on this task with more observations and a slightly different focus, as well as undertaking specific observations of individual students to observe what they do in the classroom and how much time they are active. The third week focuses more on assessment within the classroom and how this information is recorded and used by the classroom teacher. There is also a focus on the project work which is undertaken at KS4 and this requires the trainee to get to grips with the realities of what the students are doing in the classroom and the support they receive.

It is important to note that these tasks are often not directly assessed, so your question may be, why do it then? Simply put, this information can be used as part of your QTS Standards and in addition it provides the foundation which will enable you to get a better grasp of what is going on in your subject, in your school. It is all part of your individual CPD and also demonstrates to your mentor how serious you are about the course and teaching in general. Appearing to do nothing in your induction weeks simply sends a negative message to all who are about to assess you.

Written assignments

The principal method of assessing your progress and understanding other than recording the Standards for QTS status will come with the formal, assessed written assignments. The content and level at which the assignments are measured (levels 5, 6 and 7) will inevitably vary from institution to institution. However, in your final or professional year, they will usually be a combination of subject-specific assignments, for example, the role of science within secondary education, a wider cross-subject issue such as classroom management or boys' engagement, an assignment displaying your ability to plan and deliver a scheme of work and reflect upon its effectiveness and a final research-based project where you will be expected to research a topic area within your placement school and base your findings on your own research and experience as well as appropriate, relevant and recent literature.

As with all assignments, success depends upon your ability to meet the assessment criteria in terms of the content. However, as indicated earlier, time management has a huge role to play. You could, of course, wait until you have gathered all of your data together before you start to write. However, this would be a mistake. Your time will become a precious resource and leaving your assignment to the last moment is not something that you should be doing. If possible, write as you go. If you run out of time, you are not in a position to take time from your placement to write, you have classroom responsibilities which have to be addressed. Taking time off school to write assignments is clearly unprofessional and your standing with your mentor would suffer if you did this.

The message for your written assignments is clear, do not leave it to the last moment. It is therefore important to make sure that you plan out and allot time to your assignments and that you stick to your timetable. You must remember that you will be doing these assignments alongside your normal teaching activities of marking and lesson preparation, as well as gathering evidence for your QTS Standards. You need to make sure that you have enough time to collect your information, your examples, your lesson plans or whatever your assignments require. You will need to make sure that you have time to research the literature you will need to back up your points. A handy hint here is to make sure that if you use any quotes from any literature, make sure that it is correctly referenced (including page numbers if quoted as an extract i.e. over four lines long) and make sure that it is relevant for the comments you are making at the time. Do not simply plonk in a quote where it is not needed. Do not put a quote in about the importance of seating plans if you are talking about the importance of formative assessment in student progress. It's simple really!

Summary

In this chapter we have looked at some of the issues arising from the academic side of the teaching course which you are undertaking. We have seen that there are differences between the university-based assignments which you are graded on and the school-based tasks where you may not. It is important to remember that the school-based tasks, though not graded, are important due to their impact on your understanding of the school you work in and its ethos, as well as helping you understand some of the issues of teaching in a classroom. They are also a good source of evidence for the QTS Standards. Finally, we have considered the importance of time management in this whole process in terms of getting the balance right between the needs of the school and your academic progress.

15 | **What next?**

Contents

- Applying for the job
- The interview
- The NQT year

If you are reading this chapter, it's a reasonable assumption that you have navigated your way through your course, that you have managed your time well, built on your relationships, gathered the evidence for your QTS Standards, become a master at lesson planning and have flown over the hurdles of the assignments. I hope that, in some small way, this book has made the whole process easier for you. But the question must be 'what next?'

In this chapter I will look briefly at the issue of getting your first job and some of the frequently asked questions concerning your NQT Year.

Applying for the job

Applying for jobs is never an easy process, but it is something which we all have to go through. The first thing to do is to make sure that you understand very clearly the post that you are applying for and the type of school you will be working in and in both cases, you must be comfortable that you are applying to the right place. You will be investing a great deal of yourself in this post and to go to the wrong school would be an error which you will have lots of time to reflect on later on! Better to wait than rush into the first advertised post, which most of us are prone to do. There is a lot to consider here and, in addition, you may be restricted by your personal circumstances such as family commitments.

Once you have decided on the school and the post, you must then get on and make your application. It is reasonable to assume that, academically at least, candidates for the post will all be pretty much on a par. So it is the covering letter/personal statement which will make you stand out. Consequently, you should make sure that you spend a great deal of time on it, making sure that it reads well, sends the right messages and gets as close to the personal specification of the advertised post as possible. You also need to think about the structure of the document itself, it needs to flow and give the right impression from the start. If you get it wrong, you will find yourself on the 'no thanks' pile. Having consulted a number of heads of departments on this issue, I have come up with a suggested template for a good personal statement. This is divided into the following separate sections to form a seven point plan:

1. Confirm the post for which you are applying
For example:
> I would like to apply for the post of Key Stage 6 teacher at Saint Siddings School as advertised in TES, 3rd September 2010.

2. Explain what it is about the school that has attracted you
For example:
> I am particularly interested in applying to Saint Siddings because of its high reputation for involvement in the local community and its commitment to promoting individual learning of its pupils.

3. Explain what you have been doing in teaching so far
For example:
> During my teaching practice, I worked closely with a mixed Y5 and Y6 class, teaching across a range of subjects. I was particularly happy with cross-curricular project linking geography, science and ICT which I took responsibility for.

4. Target something from the advert to say what you can offer
For example:
> I note from your advert that the school is recognized for its sporting prowess. As a qualified netball coach, I would welcome the opportunity to contribute to this aspect of the school.

5. What excites you about teaching?
For example:
> I have wanted a career in teaching for as long as I can remember. Working with students while on placement has reinforced this desire. I have found that enabling students to reach their potential is the most rewarding aspect of this profession.

6. What else can you offer teaching?
For example:
> In my spare time one of my main hobbies is photography. If successful in my application, I would like to offer an after-school activity which would enable others to take up photography.

7. What makes you stand out from the other candidates?
For example:
> I feel that I am a likely and committed individual who is willing to give my all to this post. I believe that I meet all of the requirements of the personal specification and can offer more via my commitment

to extra-curricular activities. I feel that my skills in (e.g. xxx) would also be of benefit to the school. I hope to meet you in person in the near future and would welcome the opportunity to discuss these issues further.

These are simple pointers but the important thing to make sure is that your application demonstrates that you can do the job that you applied for. If you have industrial experience which may also be of benefit that's great, and you may wish to direct the reader towards this, but remember that you are applying for a teaching post so make sure the statement shows this.

The following more detailed example of a sample personal statement is a real application but clearly individual names have been removed to maintain anonymity.

Sample personal statement

I wish to apply for the position of Teacher of ICT, as advertised on the *Times Educational Supplement* website. I was attracted to your school because of its outstanding reputation and the evident dedication that it has shown to pupils and staff in learning as a lifelong experience. I was impressed with the outstanding curriculum the school offers its students and the general ethos of your school that I gleaned from your website. I feel that I possess the skills, knowledge and expertise required to fill the roles needed at Domdidom Sports College.

I am currently undertaking my PGCE in Secondary Education ICT at Sheffield Hallam University. During my time on the PGCE course, both at university and while on placement, I have been directed and instructed on how to produce meaningful and relevant learning objectives, outcomes and related resources, in order to deliver appropriate and successful lessons. I believe that during my teaching experience, I have achieved this by developing lesson plans that adhere to the KS3 National Strategy (i.e. the 3-part lesson) and, where possible, applying this to KS4 lessons. I believe that in order to effectively achieve the aims and values of the National Curriculum and for pupils to fulfil the lesson outcomes that I have set them, it is necessary to break down lessons into bite-size chunks. I have developed these skills further by creating schemes of work for AS Applied ICT courses currently being trialled at my second teaching practice.

My Initial placement took place at Doodle School, Mansfield, which is a mixed comprehensive of approximately 750 11–16-year-olds. While at Doodle School I was able to observe and put into practice a number of teaching strategies. For example, with a mixed ability Year 7 group and bottom set Year 9 group I found that pupil interaction with the whiteboard was successful and an excellent method of formative assessment. In practical lessons I would ask the pupils to describe how they performed certain tasks and then asking others to come up and demonstrate on the whiteboard. Pupils often demonstrated sophisticated and complex ICT skills and I was particularly impressed by pupils who were identified as having a lower ability or special educational needs. As a result, I also believe this to be a good method of differentiation, as quite often less able pupils find it difficult to put into words how they have achieved something, and find it easier and less daunting to show you. The utilization of this strategy gave me a clearer picture when marking and moderating their module assignments.

While on placement I was given the opportunity to teach a range of ICT subjects across KS3 and KS4. During my first placement at Doodle I was fortunate to teach both OCR Nationals and Edexcel GCSE qualifications at KS4. I particularly enjoyed teaching KS4 as I was given the chance to build my own schemes of work for my Year 11 class. I created a 4-week plan for OCR Unit 8 'Technological Innovations' and chose the subject of 'Biometric Technology'. Planning my own scheme of work allowed me to attempt new teaching strategies, for example, I identified that the school gave students little chance to develop their presentation skills needed for further education. After the unit was completed the students were required to give a 5–10-minute presentation to the rest of the class. I found that this activity motivated the students to complete their work to a high standard and within lesson time. This activity was also used to help assess the students' understanding of the unit. The students found the subject challenging, though the resources I created gave them a clear structure and progression framework. All students were able to reach their target grades and many exceeded expectations. The scheme of work and resources were then used successfully by other teachers within the department.

During my second teaching placement I was fortunate to have access to a contrasting curriculum. A quarter of my teaching timetable was dedicated to KS5. I enjoy working with A-level groups as I believe I am able to apply my own industry knowledge to my lessons. I have also had the opportunity to work in other subject areas. During my second teaching practice I have been teaching BTEC construction to a group of academically underachieving boys. I was able to apply my ICT skills to construction by simulating wall-building methods using graphic software.

My teaching placements also allowed me to give something back to the pupils. I was involved in helping many extra-curricular activities including the Choir, Christmas drama production, trampolining, podcasting, cultural art festivals and ICT coursework clubs. During my placements I endeavoured to be an integral member of the ICT departments. I also ensured that I taught in a manner that was consistent with school and departmental policies; attended departmental and LEA meetings during which future planning of lessons and marking techniques were discussed and agreed upon.

Before studying for my PGCE I completed a BSc (Hons) degree in Business and Technology at Sheffield Hallam University. The course gave me the opportunity to undertake a one-year professional placement practice, which I completed at the internet service provider Plusnet PLC. While working for Plusnet I was responsible for the company's hardware distribution, overseeing the logistics involved to ensure hundreds of broadband customers received their hardware each day. This role also required me to make multi-million pound decisions sourcing hardware from new suppliers.

I have a sociological view towards educational institutions. From my own experiences of going through the education system I feel positive reinforcement and positive labelling are key contributors towards a child's approach to learning. I come from an economically deprived background where going to university is extremely rare, so I know how much difference one teacher or school can make to a child's development. I would like to share my life experiences through my teaching and motivate others like myself to reach for goals they didn't think or were told were not possible. Teaching is a career I am extremely passionate about. I feel confident I have all the assets you are looking for and hope I can bring my enthusiasm of ICT to Domdodom Sports College.

Yours faithfully,

The interview

The next traumatic experience is the interview. Do not expect the interview to be a short one – it is more likely to take the whole day and be a series of events, not simply a 'turn up and talk'. Another thing to remember is that you will be on interview all day, wherever you are, whether you are in a formal or informal situation. So take great care. You will be amazed at how quickly a throwaway comment made during lunch will make it back from the staffroom to the interview panel. You can expect to be interviewed by a panel of teachers, probably including a member of the governors. You can also expect to have an observed teaching session, the topic of which you will have been given in advance to make sure that you are able to plan well, and you may be interviewed by some of the student body. You should also expect to have a tour of the school.

The advice for how to conduct yourself on the day should be self-evident. However, I think that it is appropriate to go over this, just to make sure. As indicated earlier in this book, how you choose to project yourself is dictated by your appearance, so dressing in an appropriate manner is vital as it is the first thing that the interview panel will see. So remember, dress to impress. Second, make sure that you maintain good eye contact at all times, smile a lot and be positive, this will set the tone for when you are in the interview. Make sure that you come across as approachable and willing to communicate. If you are too standoffish and quiet, the people you meet will wonder if there is a problem. Make sure that you ask questions when you are being taken around the school, as this makes it clear that you are very interested in the post. Make sure that the lesson you are asked to teach is not only appropriate for the group but that it demonstrates your understanding of teaching and learning. By this, I mean make sure that you have differentiated tasks, that you attempt to address different learning styles, that your teaching is stimulating and engaging. I would also recommend that you produce a secondary lesson plan which explains where this lesson would go if you had more time (you may only be given 30 minutes) and make sure that the observer sees this document.

When you go into the interview room, make sure that you greet the members of the panel appropriately then wait to be asked before you sit down. In the interview itself, make sure that your body language remains open, that you look directly at the person who is asking you questions and that you answer to the panel as a whole. Try to remain as calm as possible. The panel are aware that you are nervous and they may well feel the same way. Do not be afraid to ask an interviewer to clarify or explain a question. It is much better to understand the question than give the wrong answer. When the panel have run through their questions, they will ask you if you have any questions to ask them. Make sure that you do have a question for them. Before you will have applied for the post, it is reasonable to assume that you will have done some research into the school, usually via the school's website. As a result of this, you should have a good understanding of the school and be in a good position to ask a question about it, especially if this question has little to do with the general discussions you have had so far. It will help to show that you have been doing your homework. Once you have completed the interview, thank the panel for their time and make sure you exit in the same positive, confident manner you came into the room.

The NQT year

Many trainees get their first job before they complete the course. It is not uncommon for trainees to get appointments in the school where they have been practising but the move from a trainee to an NQT is a large one and you still have to pass this year to become a fully qualified teacher. You will still be required to gather evidence of your progress in much the same way as you did with your QTS file on your teaching practice. The biggest shift now is in terms of your co-workers' expectations of you. You will no longer be a student; you will be a fellow professional and expected to function without the same level of support which you enjoyed during your placements. Your timetable will also go up in terms of hours, leaving you less time to plan. You may be expected to take the responsibility of a form tutor as well. Your newly learnt time management skills will be hugely important to you and you have to get on top and keep on top. I can reassure you that, even though this is hard at the start, it does get easier. However, do not make the mistake of thinking that you have to do this by yourself. If you are struggling, let someone know immediately so the support can be put in place for you. Most schools have a member of staff whose responsibility it is to support NQTs and this is usually the same person who is responsible for the trainee teachers. It is in no one's interest if a teacher is unable to keep up to speed with marking or teaching and everyone needs help at times. I cannot stress enough the importance of being proactive if you need help, as it is crucial for all concerned.

This would seem to end the book on something of a low note but this is not really the case. I am always keen to let people know of the possible problems they may face in order to forewarn them – and as they say forewarned is forearmed. I have never regretted a single day of my teaching career. The rewards are huge in return for the investment you put in. Everyone who reads this book has their teachers to thank for giving them the knowledge that they have now. Everyone reading this book will be able to think of a teacher or group of teachers who have influenced them and the way they think and interact with the world. You will work with hundreds of different people and experience the joy of seeing a child understand a difficult concept, of receiving your first Christmas card, of someone accidentally calling you mum or dad which simply shows how relaxed and confident they are in your presence. You will also experience the heartbreak when they leave your school. But remember, they will take something of you with them where ever they go. I truly believe that teaching is an honour and a privilege, so make the most of the trust that has been placed in you and enjoy your career as a teacher.

Appendix: The QTS Standards

Professional Attributes

Relationships with children and young people

Q1 Have high expectations of children and young people including a commitment to ensuring that they can achieve their full educational potential and to establishing fair, respectful, trusting, supportive and constructive relationships with them.

Q2 Demonstrate the positive values, attitudes and behaviour they expect from children and young people.

Frameworks

Q3 (a) Be aware of the professional duties of teachers and the statutory framework within which they work.

(b) Be aware of the policies and practices of the workplace and share in collective responsibility for their implementation.

Communicating and working with others

Q4 Communicate effectively with children, young people, colleagues, parents and carers.

Q5 Recognise and respect the contribution that colleagues, parents and carers can make to the development and well-being of children and young people and to raising their levels of attainment.

Q6 Have a commitment to collaboration and co-operative working.

Personal and professional development

Q7 (a) Reflect on and improve their practice, and take responsibility for identifying and meeting their developing professional needs.

(b) Identify priorities for their early professional development in the context of induction.

Q8 Have a creative and constructively critical approach towards innovation, being prepared to adapt their practice where benefits and improvements are identified.

Q9 Act upon advice and feedback and be open to coaching and mentoring.

Professional knowledge and understanding

Teaching and learning

Q10 Have a knowledge and understanding of a range of teaching, learning and behaviour management strategies and know how to use and adapt them, including how to personalise learning and provide opportunities for all learners to achieve their potential.

Assessment and monitoring

Q11 Know the assessment requirements and arrangements for the subjects/curriculum areas in the age ranges they are trained to teach, including those relating to public examinations and qualifications.

Q12 Know a range of approaches to assessment, including the importance of formative assessment.

Q13 Know how to use local and national statistical information to evaluate the effectiveness of their teaching, to monitor the progress of those they teach and to raise levels of attainment.

Subjects and curriculum

Q14 Have a secure knowledge and understanding of their subjects/curriculum areas and related pedagogy to enable them to teach effectively across the age and ability range for which they are trained.

Q15 Know and understand the relevant statutory and non-statutory curricula, frameworks, including those provided through the National Strategies, for their subjects/curriculum areas, and other relevant initiatives applicable to the age and ability range for which they are trained.

Literacy, numeracy and ICT

Q16 Have passed the professional skills tests in numeracy, literacy and information and communication technology (ICT).

Q17 Know how to use skills in literacy, numeracy and ICT to support their teaching and wider professional activities.

Achievement and diversity

Q18 Understand how children and young people develop and that the progress and well-being of learners are affected by a range of developmental, social, religious, ethnic, cultural and linguistic influences.

Q19 Know how to make effective personalised provision for those they teach, including those for whom English is an additional language or who have special educational needs or disabilities, and how to take practical account of diversity and promote equality and inclusion in their teaching.

Q20 Know and understand the roles of colleagues with specific responsibilities, including those with responsibility for learners with special educational needs and disabilities and other individual learning needs.

Health and well-being

Q21 (a) Be aware of current legal requirements, national policies and guidance on the safeguarding and promotion of the well-being of children and young people.

(b) Know how to identify and support children and young people whose progress, development or well-being is affected by changes or difficulties in their personal circumstances, and when to refer them to colleagues for specialist support.

Professional skills

Planning

Q22 Plan for progression across the age and ability range for which they are trained, designing effective learning sequences within lessons and across a series of lessons and demonstrating secure subject/curriculum knowledge.

Q23 Design opportunities for learners to develop their literacy, numeracy and ICT skills.

Q24 Plan homework or other out-of-class work to sustain learners' progress and to extend and consolidate their learning.

Teaching

Q25 Teach lessons and sequences of lessons across the age and ability range for which they are trained in which they:

(a) use a range of teaching strategies and resources, including e-learning, taking practical account of diversity and promoting equality and inclusion;

(b) build on prior knowledge, develop concepts and processes, enable learners to apply new knowledge, understanding and skills and meet learning objectives;

(c) adapt their language to suit the learners they teach, introducing new ideas and concepts clearly, and using explanations, questions, discussions and plenaries effectively;

(d) manage the learning of individuals, groups and whole classes, modifying their teaching to suit the stage of the lesson.

Assessing, monitoring and giving feedback

Q26 (a) Make effective use of a range of assessment, monitoring and recording strategies.

(b) Assess the learning needs of those they teach in order to set challenging learning objectives.

Q27 Provide timely, accurate and constructive feedback on learners' attainment, progress and areas for development.

Q28 Support and guide learners to reflect on their learning, identify the progress they have made and identify their emerging learning needs.

Reviewing teaching and learning

Q29 Evaluate the impact of their teaching on the progress of all learners, and modify their planning and classroom practice where necessary.

Learning environment

Q30 Establish a purposeful and safe learning environment conducive to learning and identify opportunities for learners to learn in out of school contexts.

Q31 Establish a clear framework for classroom discipline to manage learners' behaviour constructively and promote their self-control and independence.

Team working and collaboration

Q32 Work as a team member and identify opportunities for working with colleagues, sharing the development of effective practice with them.

Q33 Ensure that colleagues working with them are appropriately involved in supporting learning and understand the roles they are expected to fulfil.

Index

absence 86
abuse of authority 86
access
    internet 123–4
action planning 60
adults
    learning styles 95
advice
    acting on 78
alcohol abuse 86
'all, most, some' approach 100
appeal process 88
appointments
    in school time 12
assessment
    importance of 112
    motivation 113–14
    school-based tasks 130–1
    teaching practice 22
    understanding methods of 79–80
    written 113–14
Assessment for Learning (AfL)
    112–13
assignments
    coping with 129–36
    failing 72
    issues with 130
    prioritization 130
    time management 130
    written 135–6
auditory learning style 96

BEd students
    difference between PGCE students
        and 72
behaviour
    recognising acceptable 80
behaviour management 80–2, 81
    training sessions 26
behaviour policy 81
body language 77
breach of confidence 86

breakout points 103–6
Bruner, Jerome 95

carers
    communicating with 77
catchment area
    knowledge of 16
'cause for concern' (C4C) document
        22, 82–5
    example of 83–5
child care 41
children
    communicating with 76
    learning styles 95
    understanding environment of 80
classroom
    use of ICT in 122
classroom assistants 3
classroom management
    ICT suite 124–6
coaching
    openness to 78–9
colleagues
    communicating with 76
    relationship with 24–5
    socialisation with 25
collective responsibility 31
comments
    avoiding negative 114–15
    length of 116
communication 12, 76–8
    body language 77
    university tutor 23
computer facilities
    hardwired 124
confidentiality 77–8
    reflective journals 53
    reflective partners 51
conflict of interests
    mentor 21
connect, activate, demonstrate,
        consolidate model 101–3

content filters
  internet 123
continuing assessment
  teaching practice 73–4
critical friend
  role of 72
critical reflection 52–4
cumulative misconduct 86
curriculum requirements
  lesson planning 108

damage to property 86
data sticks 124
delivery cycle
  lessons 108
discussion
  class 103–4
dishonesty 86
dress
  standard of 9–10, 77
  suitability for interview 141–2
drug abuse 86

educators
  definition 3–4
emails 124
encouragement
  marking and 114–15
environment
  establishing positive working 80
  understanding child's 80
equality of status
  reflective partners 52
evaluation
  lesson plans 106–9
Every Child Matters
  understanding importance of 80
expectations 14–15
experience
  learning from 49–50
extension activities 104
extra curricular activities 24
eye contact
  during interview 142

Facebook 11
failure
  analysis of 71
  appealing against 88
  assignments 72
  dealing with 70–88

mentors and 71
placement 22, 73–5
planning 81
QTS Standards 73
reasons for 74–5
falsification of records 86
feedback 45
  formative and summative reviews
    58–60
  lesson observation 67
  negative 59
  reflective cycle 68
fighting 86
first impressions
  interview 142
first jobs 137–43
formative and summative reviews
    55–61
  action planning 60
  content of 56
  feedback 58–60
  layout of review document 57
  preparation for 57–8
  purpose of 56
  role of mentor in 57
  targets 59–60
  timescale for 56
formative assessment
  summative assessment compared
    112
fraud 86

gender
  lesson planning 97
gifted and talented (G&T)
  lesson plans incorporating 97
good practice
  identifying and sharing 119–20
grading
  policy on 115–16
Graduate Teacher Programme (GTP)
    72
gross misconduct 85–6
  definition 86
groupings 81

head teacher
  induction by 17
health and safety
  ICT suite 125
hobbies 41

homework
  planning 30
honesty
  reflective partners 52

ICT
  kinaesthetic learning style and 122
  lesson planning and 122–3
  QTS Standards test 32
  use in classroom 121–7, 122
ICT suite
  classroom management in
    124–6
  health and safety issues 125
  room layout 125
  seating plan 125
  summary plenary sessions 126
incapacity 86
individuals
  working with 117–19
induction 17
information
  allocated school 15–16
information gathering
  internet 123–4
ink
  colour for marking 113
insubordination 86
internet
  access to 123–4
  content filters 123
  information gathering from 123–4
  use of in preparation 38
interpersonal skills 47
interview 141–2
  dress for 141–2
  first impressions 142
  interview panel 141
  length of 141

jeans 9
jewellery 10
job application 137–43

kinaesthetic learning style 95–6
  ICT and 122

language 10
  care with 24
lateness 86
learning

difference between teaching and
  94–5
learning styles 95
  types of 95–6
lesson
  objectives of 100
lesson observation 63–5
  concerns over 65–6
  feedback 67
  role of mentor 66
  student teacher 65–6
  visit from tutor 68–9
lesson observation sheet 64
lesson planning 81, 91–109
  breakout points 103
  connect, activate, demonstrate,
    consolidate model 101–3
  curriculum requirements 108
  importance of 93
  national specifications 108
  pre-planning 96–7
  task setting 99–100
  time-defined sessions 103
  use of ICT 122–3
lesson planning sheet
  example of 98–9
lesson plans 38
  adjusting 104
  elements of good 93–4
  evaluation 106–9
  flexibility 103–4
  incorporating breakout points
    105–6
  lesson-by-lesson approach 81
  linking lesson to 100–1
  objectives and outcomes 94
  refining 93
  relationship with scheme of work
    94
  SEN and 93
  submission to mentor 81
  university style 81
  variations in 93–4
  what to include 97–9
lesson-by-lesson approach
  lesson plans 81
lessons
  delivery cycle 108
literacy
  adequacy of 71
  QTS Standards test 32

local environment
  visiting as source of information on
    allocated school 16
local press
  source of information on allocated
    school 16
location
  reflective partners 52

managed learning environments
  (MLEs) 126
marking 38
  encouragement in 114–15
  grading 115–16
  purpose of 113–14
  technique for 114–16
meeting
  mentor 22
mentor
  'cause for concern' (C4C) document
    and 82
  conflict of interests 21
  contacting at allocated school 16
  lesson observation 66
  meetings with 22
  planning and 81
  professionalism 22–3
  QTS Standards responsibility 29–30
  relationship with 20–3
  responsibilities 21
  role in formative and summative
    reviews 57
  submission of lesson plans to 81
  visit from tutor and 68
mentoring
  acting on 78
  openness to 78–9
mentors
  failure and 71
misconduct 74
mistakes 26–7
monitors
  switching off when teacher
    addressing class 125
motivation
  assessment for 113–14

national specifications
  lesson planning 108
network control software 126
networks 124

non-teaching staff
  relationship with 25–6
NQT year 59, 142–3
numeracy
  adequacy of 71
  QTS Standards test 32

objectives
  lesson plans 94
  lessons 100
  reviewing 101
observation
  concerns over 65–6
  feedback 67
  reasons for 107
  reflective cycle 68
  student teacher 65-6
  teaching by others 63–5
  visit from tutor 68–9
OFSTED
  as source of information on
    schools 16
out-of-class work
  planning 30
outcomes
  lesson plans 94

parents
  communicating with 77
peer assessment 119–20
personal information 11
personal statement
  sample 139–41
  template for 138
PGCE students 35
  differences between BEd students
    and 72
physical contact 24
placement
  avoiding close to home 15
  failing 73–5
  number of 73
  reasons for failure 74–5
  variations in 73
planning
  failure of 81
  mentor and 81
policies
  implementing 31
pre-planning
  lesson planning 96–7

pre-starter activities 101
preparation 37–8
prioritization
  assignments 130
problems 26–7
professional attributes
  formative and summative
    reviews 57
professional development
  taking responsibility for 78
Professional Knowledge and
    Understanding Standards 80
  formative and summative
    reviews 57
Professional Skills
  formative and summative reviews
    57
Professional Skills and Understanding
    59
professionalism
  communication 12
  definition 8–9
  dress 9–10
  language 10
  mentor 22–3
  outside school 10–11
  QTS 8–9
  reflective practice 47–8
  social networking 11
  timekeeping 11–12
Prom Night
  disruption caused by 122
Public Interest (Disclosure) Act (1998)
    86

Qualified Teacher Status (QTS)
    Standards 5, 22, 28–33
  definition 29
  electronic collection of quality
    evidence 29
  failing 73
  meeting 75
  mentors responsibility for 29–30
  professionalism 8–9
  proof of meeting 75
  quality evidence 29–32
  structure 29
  tests 32–3
quality evidence
  displaying 31
  electronic collection of 29

QTS Standards 29–32
  to reference more than one QTS
    Standard 32
questions
  asking during interview 142
quotes
  use of in written assignments 136

racial offences 86
referencing
  written assignments 136
reflection
  as learning tool 46–9
  writing up 53–4
reflective cycle
  observation and feedback 68
reflective journals 46, 52–3
reflective partners 50–1
  ground rules for 51–2
  identifying 51
reflective practice 45–55
  definition 45
  importance of 45–6
  practical application 49–50
  reflective cycle 48–9
register
  taking 101
relationships 20–7
relatives
  in placement schools 15
resources 66
  development 38, 81
responsibility
  accepting 26
review document
  layout of 57
review meeting 59
risk management 24
room layout
  ICT suite 125

Saying 'no' 39
schemes of work 108
  relationship with lesson plan 94
school
  allocation of 15
  contacting allocated 16
  finding information on allocated
    15–16
  time management 36–7
  travelling to allocated 16–17, 37

school (*Contd.*)
  website as source of information on
    allocated 16
school mentor 3
school-based tasks
  assessment 130–1
  examples of 131–5
schools
  experiencing range of 73
seating plan
  ICT suite 125
seating plans 81
self-assessment 119–20
self-awareness 46
SENCO
  induction by 17
senior liaison tutor 3
  induction by 17
skirts
  length of 10
small groups
  working with 117–19
smoking on premises where
    prohibited 86
social networking 11
socialisation
  colleagues 25
space to think
  reflective partners 52
special educational needs (SEN)
  lesson plans incorporating
    93, 97
  training sessions 26
staff
  size of 25
starter activity
  function of 101
statistical information
  use of 31
statutory framework
  teaching duties 31–2
Steer Report (2009) 81, 93
student-friendly language 100
students
  assessing work of 110–20
  avoiding going into room alone
    with 24
  avoiding physical contact 24
  child care 41
  relationship with 23–4
subject knowledge 79

summary plenary sessions 101
  ICT suite 126
summative assessment
  formative assessment compared 112
support staff 4
  relationship with 25–6
swearing 10

targets
  formative and summative reviews
    59–60
task setting 99–100
teaching
  difference between learning and
    94–5
  observation 63–5
teaching environment
  experiencing different 73
teaching practice
  assessments of 22
  balancing with university work
    39–41
  continuing assessment 73–4
  creating right impression 17
  expectations 14–15
  failure of placement 22
  practical issues 15
  preparing for 13–18
teaching styles
  differences in 95
technicians 4
  relationship with 25
teenage crushes
  dealing with 26–7
test centres
  QTS Standards tests 32
tests
  QTS Standards 32–3
theft 86
ties 10
time
  reflective partners 52
time management 35–43
  assignments 130
  definition 35
  importance of 35–6
  improving 36
  organizing the day 39
  written assignments 136
time-defined sessions 103
timekeeping 11–12

timetables 37
trainee teachers
    expectation of pupils 97
    relationship with other 26
Training and Development Agency for
    Schools (TDA)
    help with gathering quality
        evidence 29
training sessions
school-based 26
tutor
    requirements for visit from 69
    visit from 68–9

uniform 9–10
Uniform Resource Locator (URL) 124
university tutor
    communication with 23
    relationship with 23
university work
    balancing with teaching practice
        39–41

verbal motivation 116–17
violence 86

virtual learning environments (VLEs)
    40, 124
    use of 126–7
visit from tutor 68–9
    requirements for 69
visual learning style 96

WALT (What are We Learning Today)
    100
websites
    source of information on allocated
        school 16
WILF (What am I Looking For) 100
withdrawal
    from course 86–7
    temporary 87
work-life balance 41–2
written assessments 113–14
written assignments 135–6
    referencing 136
    time management 136
    use of quotes in 136

young people
    communication with 76